The Sign of the Ivory Horn

Eastern African Civilizations

by
Ricky Rosenthal

1971
OCEANA PUBLICATIONS, INC.
Dobbs Ferry, New York

Library of Congress Catalog Card Number: 70-132279

International Standard Book Number: 0-379-00449-6

Manufactured in the United States of America

ACKNOWLEDGEMENTS

To the Shomburg Collection, of the New York Public Library, to the American Geographical Society, and the Department of Egyptology of the Brooklyn Museum for their special services, I am very grateful. To the Dag Hammarskjold Library of the United Nations, and to my colleague Ted Morello for his guidance and invaluable assistance. To all my African friends at the United Nations who sparked my interest originally, and continued to encourage me adding their own special insight and enthusiasm, I am indebted.

R.R.

CONTENTS

Contents (continued)

LIST OF ILLUSTRATIONS

INTRODUCTION

"The history of East Africa is only the history of
its invaders . . . The East Africans are a great black
background to the comings and goings of brown men
and white men on the coast."

Sir Reginald Coupland

Meroe, Zimbabwe, Monomotapa--all were African civilizations in the forefront of history, not just the great "black background" for the "comings and goings" of other races.

The wholly wrong conception that Black Africa developed
from the coasts inward was the product of wishful thinking by outsiders. Europeans wanted to believe that foreign influences provided Africa with stunning achievements. Europeans could not
accept that African societies from the earliest times were organized along African lines that filled African needs and inclina-
tions, that they were shaped by African conceptions of the world
and that many of these societies were pre-Christian and pre-
Moslem.

Through the long march of man's evolution, Africa has remained at the very center of the inhabited world. It is, indeed,
the cradle of man. Early men have been found to have lived in
China and Indonesia; but the earliest known cultural product--
authentic "pebble tools, "a crude chopping tool flaked from a stone
or pebble to form a cutting edge--are an African discovery with
the center of distribution in the woodland savanna regions of tropical Africa. The archaeological record suggests that there is a
continuous indigenous development in Africa rather than a suc-
cession of external impacts by other peoples. The palaeontalogical
record makes it very clear that Caucasoid types were not invaders

1

but were resident in East Africa from the remotest times.

In studying African history, a geographical framework is of immense use and relevance in the light of the fact that we owe such new data as has emerged to the art and science of archaeology. Ecological differences can prevent or provoke trade and the spread of ideas. For example, the area along the Nile Valley, in particular the part of the river directly north of Khartoum and further south, is suited to receiving traits and passing them along the main Nile. Meroe was admirably situated for just such cosmic cultural purposes. To the west of the Khartoum area is the savanna country which stretches with its own climactic personality across the African continent. Traits and peoples moved freely back and forth along both of these routes: river and savanna.

There are enormous difficulties in deducing social organization from archaeological finds. The last 25 years have seen a growing interest in African archaeology, but lack of funds and a low density of archaeologists make some of the information both tentative and fragmentary. This in no way diminishes its value; it is merely a realistic description of the intensity but sparseness of scientific work at this time.

It is hoped that the clamor from outside for African studies programs will provide a stimulus for this vital groundwork. The study of African history is a humbling one, for here the sweep of man's evolution can be surveyed along with his biological success in the struggle for survival.

Archaeological investigation still remains the historian's basic tool for probing into the past that predates the advent of written records. Bone, antler and shell are preserved through time; but flesh, sinew, hide and animal fibers are more perishable. In man's struggle to survive, he achieved a capacity to make clothes, tools, houses--in short, the whole content of the archaeological record.

Africa is particularly rewarding for those who are engaged in its study because, in isolated cases, it has peoples who still are practicing a prehistoric culture almost unsullied by the scars of industrialization. Some of today's Bantu-speaking peoples are survivals of early Iron Age cultures. Because it is a study in its own right, I have only touched upon the Iron Age in Africa, for it is a highly specific aspect of the last 2,000 years of African prehistory. The Iron Age is an important arena because during this time agriculture, ironworking and pastoralism were introduced. The African Iron Age is contemporary with the time at which men of European and Mediterranean civilizations were voyaging beyond their frontiers; those who sailed to Africa left accounts of their observations and exploits which can be used to amplify and supplement the testimony of archaeological sources. The Arab travelers provided one such added source. In the middle of the first millennium A.D., Masudi and Edrisi made invaluable descriptive and historical contributions. Portuguese domination of East Africa is well documented. And although Portuguese sources are not completely unbiased, they are a rich variant along with the anthropological study of local traditions. Thus, while Monomotapa is well documented through 17th-century Portuguese eyes, in tracing the history of the Shona and Rozwi peoples we draw heavily upon linguistic and social anthropology.

Oral history is of immense value to the expert, and some oral history extends reliably as far back as 300 years. This kind of history has a decisive if limited use. Such ethnohistorians as D.P. Abraham have been able to reconstruct complete sequences for periods of over 500 years by coordinating the use of Portuguese documents and the histories told to him by today's Shona people. Other implements which help to weave together loose threads into the African historical fabric are ethnobotany, paleontology, physical anthropology, physics, zoology, serology, Iron Age archaeology, dendrochronology, the history of food crops and the pattern of settlement.

The study of pottery is of first importance in reconstructing African history. Pottery is the most common artifact found at post-Stone Age sites. Iron objects tend to disintegrate in soils that are acidic, as African soils are; and gold is found only in Rhodesia and West Africa. Copper and its alloys were not generally used in Eastern Africa.

Why is the study of pottery of such high importance? A few examples drawn from field experience will illustrate the value of these remnants from the past. Pastoral peoples of the same culture, for example, will make pottery in a restricted range of forms. More settled peoples will produce a wide range of sizes and shapes. The simple cooking pot or bowl is basic. It often has a rim that can be gripped and a round base that can be wedged between the stones of a hearth. Another example would be the water jar, which has a narrow neck to cut down evaporation and to reduce the risk of spillage. Such functional forms are basic to agricultural societies. If such a vessel is absent, it suggests that the people used gourds or leather bags in which to carry their water; one might then infer that the lighter, less fragile containers belonged to nomads or a similarly less sedentary people.

The settled agriculturalists are much better represented in the archaeological record than are the simpler pastoral peoples. The migrant slash-and-burn agriculturalist or the pottery-using hunter is not so well represented because his effects are destroyed as he moves from place to place. An agricultural society will have more diverse forms of pottery and perhaps supply the pastoral people with motifs that are more decorative. Moving as they must, the pastoral peoples carry these borrowed styles from place to place. In this way, they diffuse the design, and subsequently others produce pottery of their own in imitation.

The absence of pottery kilns in present-day ethnographic studies shows that all pottery was made in open fires and that a large variety of fuels was used. The origin of pottery in East Africa is a problem in the study of the region's history. It is now assumed that pottery, which was antedated by basketry, was "invented" by accident. It is thought that when clay was being smeared on the inside of baskets, as it is to keep such small contents as seeds from slipping through, a mud-smeared basket was inadvertently dropped into a fire.

The area which peoples select to organize their settlements is of the greatest interest, for in this choice are the limits and expressions of their everyday life. For example, at Zimbabwe the construction, shape and use of materials reveal the nature of the inhabitants who lived there. The living quarters of the people within the mighty walls of Zimbabwe were not merely shelters or places to sleep and eat but significant in every detail. Thus, the position of the hearth or the door may express a traditional belief.

Early dwellings are complex and are the product of many techniques worked out and modified by peoples' own experiences. A wattle, wood or turf building is usually far from "simple," as some may characterize it. Technological skill, the tools available and the environment play a large part in the determination of a house's form and function. The rate of decay in the tropics is a stern taskmaster and dictates that any building is usually of a temporary character--the exception, of course, being construction in stone, which is rare in Africa. The communal habits of a people also have a role in determining the design of structures. Also, opportunity to imitate dwellings from more advanced cultures is important in assessing the whole.

In other words, the technological aspects cannot be appreciated without some reference to the social and natural setting of the inhabitants.

Moving forward in time to another chapter in east coast history, we find that architectural diversity becomes a crucial element in the study of Africa. The imprint of the architects of Islam permeates coastal settlements and culture, which was a mixture of African and Arab elements. The architectural forms of the coast are entirely alien to the houses of the interior. The use of coral and limestone, an innovation in itself on the coast, along with the use of mangrove poles for structural timber, may be expressions of the unique African coastal personality. Glazed insets used for architectural ornamentation might be one decorative aspect of that personality confined to the coast. The palace at Kilwa is still one of the region's architectural monuments. The similarities between the dome-shape used at Kilwa and in India clearly stress the Asian subcontinent's influence. In East Africa before the 18th century, there were none of the arch forms characteristic of the architecture of Islam--the horseshoe or four-centered arches of Persia, for example.

The African past is not easy to interpret. Some parts of the continent have been visited by literate peoples for thousands of years, while other areas have lived in isolation. Materials are difficult to preserve. The acid soils are destructive to human remains, and the depth of the soils is too shallow to retain hut-pole imprints which are so helpful in temperate climates in determining where man lived. Thick vegetation hinders access, too. Roads seldom exist, and the lush growth completely obscures earthworks and mines. This thick vegetation prevents any useful aerial photography.

The Rift Valley of East Africa favors the preservation of fossils. The inland basins of the Rift Valley have always cradled lakes which have in past ages attracted Stone Age hunters. These ancient lakes, including Olduvai, have been cleft by later earth movements or drainage changes and have revealed by erosion the astounding story of man in the layers of rock. For this reason, the most minute clues must not be overlooked in the fascinating search of African history.

A heavy burden is put on potshards, which must serve to interpret the major movements of peoples, such as the extraordinary migration of the Bantu peoples from the Congo throughout Africa.

Archaeological work moves slowly from the time of the selection of sites to the major excavations. Dr. Louis Leakey prospected for 20 years in the Olduvai area before he chose excavation sites.

In the days gone by, patrons would encourage archaeologists to make "glamour" finds--that is, to discover great monuments or art objects. Emphasis was on works of art, which became the keystone to many a millionaire's private collection and a social embellishment to his wealth of interests. But there is more to life than the great art objects; for although early populations were small in comparison to today's numbers, they were composed mostly of ordinary people coping with their environment. Yet for all their numerical superiority, they are precisely the ones whose story is written most obscurely, when at all, in the archaeological record.

More and more, cultures are being studies in relation to their ecological situation. Climate and geography can be said to speed or impede cultural development. For example, many influences did not reach East Africa owing to the impassability of the Libyan, or Western, Desert, one of the most desolate parts of the Sahara. The Sudd swamps, choked with papyrus reeds on the Upper Nile, were an impediment to travel.

Climate can be crucial. In the desert, the prime factor is rainfall. Because of the very precarious nature of the subsistence way of life in the Sahara, any natural changes of even the smallest kind would have widespread effects. There is every indication that the Sahara once had more moisture. The ancient Greeks in their mythology attributed the formation of the Libyan Desert to Phaeton's ill-starred attempt to drive the chariot of the sun across the heavens. Detailed studies by Soluman Huzayyin of the Saharan climate point comclusively to almost cataclysmic changes.

"In perhaps no other area of the world have such changes (in climate, vegetation and human adjustments) been so violent, far-reaching or effective," he says.

For example, the geography of Nubia is hostile to the spontaneous growth of urban centers. The study of Nubian geography and climate would show that the natural tendency of this farming population is to disperse itself along the rivers in order to exploit all available land. Hence, the spectacular growth and prosperity of Meroe must be traced to this unique factor, among other influences.

Dividing Africa along geographic lines is useful to the detailed, often recondite work of the specialist. But for the nonexpert, African studies must be approached on a continental scale to be the satisfying subject that it is.

CHAPTER 1 IN THE BEGINNING

"Africa's contribution to the mainstream of human
culture is man."
George Gaylord Simpson

The Quaternary Period of the earth, spanning the last
1,750,000 years, was but a moment by geological standards.
Yet encompassing as it did the Pleistocene Epoch, it embraced
the critical stage in the evolution of organisms and was witness
to the growth of culture, which had the effect of clearing the path
to literacy--a development which in turn led to man's awareness
of his own unique destiny in the biological order.

Palaeontology distinguishes the major divisions of the Pleistocene, an epoch which began roughly a million years ago and
continued to 10,000 years ago. The epoch is divided into the
Lower, Middle and Upper. The Lower Pleistocene Epoch is the
most mysterious of the three, and the least is known about it in
detail. At this time, the most vital steps affecting man's biological evolution took place.

Our planet at this time was rent by great spasms, rare in
geological history. Violent climatic and environmental changes
took place. These spastic upheavals had a marked effect on human evolution, decisively affecting mammals. Some 15 glaciations occurred during the time of the Lower Pleistocene. Except
at their higher altitudes, the tropical and equatorial parts of the
world were remote from the glaciations. However, even the
regions spared the direct effects of the ice movements experienced
increased rainfall during what are called the "pluvial periods"
that were a by-product of the glaciers.

It was during the Pleistocene Epoch that man came into existence. Because the basic geography of the world was altered
during this time, the most profound influence on man, plants and

animals--indeed, on the entire ecosystem--was brought into play. So crucial is the relationship of climate to cultural development that it is thought that because the people south of the Sahara were isolated by a dry climatic phase between the fourth and first millenniums, they became cut off from North Africa and the seminal cultural influences that were taking place in that area.

It was during the East African Pleistocene that "true man separated from his man-like (now extinct) cousins, the Australopithecines, or 'near men,' of some two million years ago," says the distinguished anthropologist, Dr. Louis Leakey. The Pleistocene ended at about 8000 B.C. There is evidence that East Africa from about 5500 to 2500 B.C. went through a period of greater rainfall, known as the Makalian Wet Phase, which must have profoundly affected cultural development--either as a deterrent or as a stimulus. Some scientists speculate that it is during dry periods that the most development takes place, at least in areas where there is mixed vegetation.

By 6000 B.C., there were two main areas in which people of sub-Saharan Africa were concentrated: one group in the gallery, or mountain, forest country and the other living around water sources in the grasslands along the seacoast. The former subsequently developed root-crop cultivation, which led to cereal agriculture and animal domestication.

The Serengeti Plain of Tanzania, just west of the eastern branch of the Rift Valley, houses the Olduvai Gorge. Now a dust bowl, this area was once wetter and greener and alive with a different order of life. In this gorge, some of the most dramatic traces of the human evolutionary process have been found. Olduvai has been cleft by convulsive movements of earth. The erosion that took place in the wake of these upheavals has laid bare its strata. In these earth layers are the cultural biographies of early man. Olduvai is a veritable archive which can be read by science. The deposits unfold in a sequence that reveals fossil mammals and stone tools. The gorge represents the framework from which the prehistory of the world may be seen, and it firmly declares that Africa is the cradle of man.

On July 17, 1959, Dr. Leakey and his wife, Mary--also an archaeologist--were working at Olduvai. Leakey suddenly became ill and remained at the camp site, but his wife decided to walk about the area. She was ranging over the site, which they had designated as Bed I, when thirst and fatigue suddenly gripped her. Just as she was about to return to camp, her sharp eyes picked out a piece of bone in the process of being exposed by erosion. From its texture, she recognized it as a skull bone.

She rushed to her husband, whose illness vanished at the news. First, they photographed the site, and then they dug in. It was here in the living floor of an ancient camp site at the lowest level of Bed I that the Leakeys found Zinjanthropus, who had lived 1.7 million years before.

Dr. Leakey labeled the discovery "Zinjanthropus boisei, " or--more informally--"Zinj." The word "Zinj" or "Zanj" was the ancient name given to East Africa, and the "boisei" was intended as a tribute to Charles Boise, whose financial aid made the Leakey excavation possible.

"Zinj, " who was about 18 years old when he died, was found lying among pebbles and waste flakes. Animal bones were found, too, and identified as the remains of snakes, lizards, rodents and amphibians. An immature pig was unearthed along with antelope bones. These layers of Bed I probably were those of an old lake which had dried up; for fish, crocodile and hippopotomus fossils also were found.

Climatic changes at Olduvai can be verified through the presence of mineral structures called "roses of the desert." These are crystalline structures which are formed of calcite and found at varying depths in the Sahara Desert. The seasonal fluctuations at Olduvai are found to have been similar to those that occur in African lakes today.

While excavating in 1960, the Leakeys came upon more crude tools, which looked as though they might have been used for skinning and cutting up carcasses. Also found were hammer stones used for getting at the marrow of bones. The readings became clearer and clearer: Olduvai was revealing the time when man was switching from being a scavenger to a hunter who gradually began to live in groups and to transmit his acquired knowledge to other generations.

In February of 1961, the Leakeys again made a spectacular find--a man even earlier than "Zinj." It was the skull of a child about 12 years of age. Leakey wrote of this discovery that "we are dealing with quite a distinct type of early hominid." He called him "Homo habilis," meaning "able" or "handy" and referring to his tool-making abilities. There is much controversy surrounding the categories into which these early men fit. Included in this controversy was the extent of his intellectual powers and his technical know-how.

Zinjanthropus qualifies in every way for the designation of true man. The reason for so classifying him is that he made tools in a regular and set pattern. Tool-making is not synonymous with tool-using. Recent studies of the primates--gorillas, baboons and chimpanzees--of East Africa are casting new light on the behavior patterns and the social life of incipient tool-making and tool-using tendencies among creatures not very different from our own ancestors. These studies are helping prehistorians to evaluate anew what happened in this most fundamental human revolution when an ape-man with a brain half the size of our own crossed the threshold of human history. More than man's physical form was inherited from these pre-men. We must take into account that many of the characteristics of human behavior had their origins in the animal world.

It is clear from reading the earliest layers at Olduvai, or Bed I, that "Zinj" lived by killing young animals and eating rats, mice, large tortoises and catfish--prey which he, as well as all the other Olduvai dwellers of his time, could catch by hand. Even so, they probably rarely ate meat because of the limited number of species which could be so taken; as a result, they probably foraged for much of their food.

This earliest of our closest relatives probably lived much like the baboon, squatting to eat his food and leaving his rubbish in the form of chipped pebbles and cracked bones. As man progressed from scavenger to hunter, he learned to cooperate with his fellow man and probably made some rudimentary grunts in the process. At this stage, Zinjanthropus probably used wooden clubs to clout larger game, such as the prehistoric zebra colt.

Most of the obvious differences that set man apart from the ape came after the use of tools. The earliest tool-makers in the world were geographically from East Africa and chronologically from the latest part of the Pleistocene Epoch. Recent excavations near Lake Rudolph in Ethiopia by Richard E. Leakey, son of Louis and Mary Leakey, promise to fill some of the blank spaces in the prehistoric picture. If proven correct, the theory surrounding his finds push the scientific record back to four million years ago.

"Here lie more than a thousand square miles of sediments . . . bearing countless bones of extinct animals and, we now know, creatures akin to man," said Richard Leakey.

Jaws and teeth have been dug up at the Ethiopian site; they are so much like the Olduvai excavations that there is a feeling that the two sites may be related. Dr. Leakey himself has observed that just the framework of the history of early man exists and that 80 per cent is absent. Perhaps his son's discoveries will reduce the percentage of the unknown.

The fragmentary remains in Ethiopia relate an unexpected story, untold up to now. It can be inferred from studying the teeth, which were small, that defensive weapons must have been used some two million years before the earliest stone tools.

If proven, this hypothesis would substantially change the story of man's cultural evolution. It is known that when a tool can be used defensively, the size of the teeth diminish in the course of biological evolution. The ape does not become a man because he uses a weapon in his hand; but because the ape does, he shifts the forces of natural selection clearly in the human direction. In other words, geneticists say, the reductive mutations accumulate in the gene pool. Eventually, the gene structure that controls the direction of growth of the teeth fails to develop along the lines of its remote ancestors. As has been mentioned, the chasm that finally evolved between man and ape came after the use of tools. The whole catalogue of tools has been found in African soil, from the earliest attempts at stone-flaking a million and a half years ago to the more complicated hand-axes of about a quarter of a million years ago.

Freedom for his hands was the result of man's standing upright. There clearly was a new reality evolving for him. Darwin was correct in suggesting that tool-using is both the cause and the effect of walking upright on two legs. Even limited bipedalism left man free to use his hands for locomotor activity. The advantage this gave led to more efficient use of the legs as he continued to walk upright, looking forward to the time when man would hunt large game and would need speed, endurance and skill to chase his wounded prey. The upright stance also led to the more efficient use of tools.

The expansion of early man's world was based on his motor abilities, intelligence and emotions. This further form of evolving man was exploratory, intelligent, energetic and even playful. New behavior patterns were the impetus which led to new forms of behavior which evolved into more complex social systems. The myriads of physical traits that began to emerge subsequently was in response to the pressure of environment.

Although the first appearance of the modern Homo sapiens dates from just under 35,000 years ago, he did not declare himself in the archaeological record until about 10,000 years ago. This could never rule out the possibility that other changes of which we are completely unaware did not occur in the forest. The Negro may well be placed in time before 10,000 B.C., but there is no clear evidence of his presence until the Iron Age. The Negro originated from the Stone Age hunter and food-gatherer. The Bushman, too, evolved later as a variant of this Negroid stock in response to his environment.

The Negro stock is believed to have a close relationship to the savanna-woodland and forest regions. The oldest known representative of the Negro in East Africa was found at Khartoum, in the Republic of the Sudan, and is called the Mesolithic Khartoum. It is dated at about 7000 B.C. There was another skull found in West Africa, at Asselar, 200 miles northeast of Timbuktu, in the Republic of Mali. It is thought to be as old as the Mesolithic Khartoum, if not older.

These earliest of Negroes found thus far were the Mesolithic hunters and fishermen who had already acquired improved methods of sustaining life in the Nile region, which was well-watered at that time around Khartoum. The introduction of cereal crops was of prime historical importance to these Mesolithic populations, for it permitted them to become sedentary and to occupy permanently and more widely territory which previously had been only a place of temporary settlement. Dr. J. Desmond Clark believes that the early hoe and axe cultures were the product of the Negro peoples. As we shall see, the Khartoum area was to become the seat of Meroe, the oldest black African civilization known.

Stone Age man was a tropical mammal. The elimination of his hairy coat at a previous stage of his evolution left him with the problem of dispelling the heat through his unprotected skin. Although he was richly endowed with sweat glands, they did not screen out the dangerous ultraviolet rays of the sun. The physiological response to this dilemma was the gradual development of the protective, skin-darkening pigment called melanin. From that, one could draw the conclusion that the Middle Pleistocene man, our ancestor, was black.

The tool, which is called a nonperishable cultural element, is the standard and most characteristic of man's artifacts. Stone Age man must have lived in terror. While he hunted, the female collected food and tried to keep the children safe. For both offense and defense, this early man had only crude implements at his disposal. With his small brain, ineffectual teeth and lack of claws, he probably was deathly afraid of the deep forest and rejected the discomforts of the highlands, which were wet and cold. Life for him was full of dangers and discomforts, and technological changes for ameliorating his circumstances came remarkably slowly.

Because the prehistoric community of man is now being seen in his changing ecological setting, we can reconstruct some things by inference. For example, it is possible to engage in informed speculation on why stone tool-making first appeared in the savanna. The tropical woodlands and savannas of Africa were witness and hosts to a decisive biological, cultural and intellectual evolution in the history of man. It is thought that tool-making first appeared in the savanna in response to a deterioration of the climate, which forced early man to supplement his declining supplies of vegetation with other kinds of food. This could well be the reason that man was forced to eat meat and that he invented a sharp cutting tool, perhaps to slit an antelope skin.

The mental activity required for the planned manufacture of tools was so unlike that of man's ancestors that an analysis of the physical changes that took place to make this possible is well worth elaborating. The cortex of the brain had attained by this time a sufficient complexity of organization so that the systematic making of weapons and tools could come about.

The passing on of acquired knowledge, so essential to man's intellectual evolution, and his capacity for foresight, which is the

use of other people's past experience, are essential steps up
the ladder to more complex brain processes. The nerve cells
in the cerebral cortex have been compared to the valves of an
electronic computer. The sense organs pass on information to
the brain by a process compared to that of the calculating capacity of the computer. The mechanism solves problems and directs
suitable bodily activity through the motor cells and nerves con-
trolling the muscles. These cortical cells of the brain base their
calculations on the information received at the moment and take
into account the patterns of past activity left by experience or
memory. The coordination of past and present information,
leading to reasoning and voluntary action, is the function called
the "association area." Man's brain and that of the ape differ in
size mainly due to the expansion of the cortical parts, which are
mainly concerned with the integration through which conceptual
thought becomes possible.

The most distinctive aspect of the human brain is the large
size of the frontal and temporal lobes. There is every reason
to conclude that these are connected with the higher mental fac-
ulties. Although man's tool-making capacity has been billed as
his most wonderous accomplishment, it is his oral tradition which
is the inheritance most distinctive of man. Chimpanzees use tools
(that is, they put together natural objects such as a stick or a
blade of grass to perform a task), but they do not manufacture
anything for their own use.

There is no doubt that language has facilitated such activi-
ties as systematic tool-making. The invention of language has
been compared with that of teaching the uneducated deaf. The deaf
without education think in terms of events as a whole--not in terms
of one thing at a time which has a name or a comparable symbol.

The earliest means that man used to communicate with those
around him was gestures. There is some evidence to suggest that
these gestures generated unconscious movements of the mouth.
It is thought that as man began to make tools and became more

preoccupied with that task, this led to the change from the manual to the oral means of communication. Hunting, too, must have contributed to the development of oral communication; hunting in groups must have been the most challenging of pursuits, making a more advanced form of dialogue necessary.

Prehistoric man was entirely dependent upon his environment. His habits and his means of existence absolutely relied on his natural resources and his response to the animals and plants with which he shared his territory. The study of the fauna during the Pleistocene suggests that the large ungulates, or hoofed mammals, were more varied a million years ago than they are today. The habitat differentiation into forest, savanna and desert which exists today apparently were not markedly different then. And then as now, the grass cover of the savanna spawned rich crops of large game animals. Perhaps for that reason, the savanna seems to have provided an optimal environment for early man.

Surely the savanna of East Africa at the beginning of the Pleistocene resembled the spectacle of today, with its vast population of elephant, hippo, buffalo, topi, waterbuck, reedbuck, duiker and warthog. This great supply of protein raises interesting questions relating to the study of the human species, for the savanna must have constituted an ideal hunting terrain in which, even with his rudimentary means, man could be successful. It was here that he could find abundant food without exposing himself to the risk of hunting down the large carnivores.

It is possible that if these distant ancestors of ours had the habit of spending nights in trees, it was either for shelter or to greatly reduce the peril from wild animals. As the population of early man began to grow because of the more abundant and regular supply of nourishing food, the felids and canids must have learned to avoid this enterprising and uncommon biped who displayed a talent for competing with them.

CHAPTER 2 MEROË IN RELIEF

" . . . heaps of broken pedestals and obelisks."
James Bruce

About one hundred miles to the north of modern-day Khartoum, a distinct African Nilotic civilization arose. Called Meroë, this kingdom was rooted in African soil and nourished by both the Nile River and the intellectual silt that washed about its banks.

From the Old Kingdom onward, the Egyptians controlled these southern Nile lands, known to them as Nubia. They maintained fortresses and trading posts at Buhen. At Semna and Kumma, they fostered trade and protected the gold mines of Nubia. From Thebes, the high priests of Ammon ruled as viceroys over Nubia, called "the gold lands of Ammon."

But Egyptian power was seriously weakened near the end of the New Kingdom (ca. 1100 B.C.). It was at about this time that Libyan warrior clans began to settle along great swaths of the Nile.

Although Meroë thrived from the sixth century B.C. to the fourth century A.D., it is not certain at what point she became a fully developed Nubian kingdom. Her capital city was at Napata, whose site remains in doubt but which was situated somewhere between the fourth and fifth cataracts of the Nile.

Meroë was greatly favored by geography. She was situated on some of the most desirable pasture land in the northern Sudan and enjoyed the benefits of three great rivers: the Blue Nile, the White Nile and the Atbara. In addition, the land lay within a belt of favorable annual rainfall.

Meroë also was in an area particularly propitious for trade. For one thing, she was at the end of caravan routes from the Red Sea. For another, the natural route from east to west between the desert in the north and the forest in the south must have been used extensively through all periods of history. Lake Chad on this east-west route seems to have been an important secondary diffusion center from which ideas and culture radiated to the southwest and southeast.

North of Meroë, the Nile Valley was one of the routes along which civilization developed in the Fertile Crescent. From the Lower Nile, it made its way deeper into Africa, and from the upper valley it spread to the rest of the continent.

One stimulus which propelled Meroë into such remarkable prosperity was the abundant deposits of iron ore, along with the availability of fuel to smelt it. This combination gave the kingdom a decided technological advantage which made it capable of defending itself against attack.

Meroë did not, of course, spring into history full-blown. One of its antecedents was the Kingdom of Kush. The beginnings of Kush are remote. It perhaps dates back to early farmers who lived between the first and second cataracts and whose culture was similar to that of the pre-dynastic Egyptians. Even though the moment of Kush's birth cannot be precisely determined, we know at what point in time her history intersects that of Egypt.

The first mention of Kush appears in Egyptian records in the reign of Amenophis I during the Middle Kingdom after 2000 B.C. Amenophis noted that his armies "passed beyond Kush and reached the end of the earth"--possibly a reference to the third cataract. But he did not hold the newly invaded territory securely. Before Hyksos' invasion, sometime between 1750 and 1550 B.C. during what is called the Second Intermediate Period, the whole of Nubia managed to gain its independence. A new state emerged in the region of Kerma, south of the third cataract. It was a trading state which, among other things, fashioned a distinctive kind of pottery. Kush's ancestry may reside here.

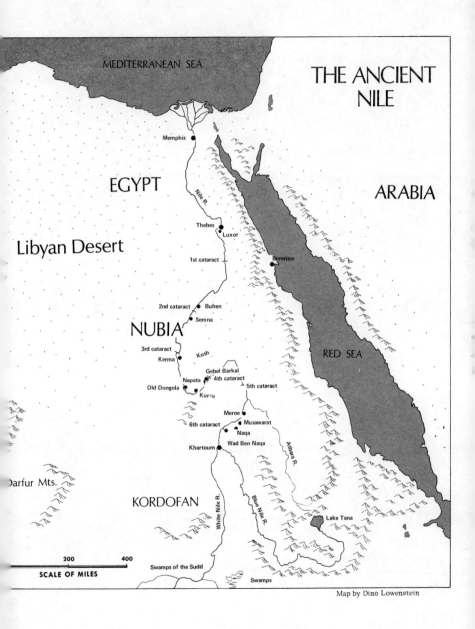

MEDITERRANEAN SEA

THE ANCIENT
NILE

EGYPT

ARABIA

Libyan Desert

Memphis

Nile R.

Thebes
Luxor

1st cataract

Berenice

2nd cataract   Buhen
                Semna

NUBIA

3rd cataract
Kerma   Kush

                Gebel Barkal
            Napata   4th cataract
Old Dongola   5th cataract
            Kurru

RED SEA

                Meroe
    6th cataract   Musawarat
                Naqa
Khartoum   Wad Ben Naqa

Atbara R.

Darfur Mts.

KORDOFAN

White Nile R.

Blue Nile R.

Lake Tana

200   400

SCALE OF MILES

Swamps of the Sudd

Swamps

Map by Dino Lowenstein

Expeditions into southern Nubia were renewed with the end of Hyksos and the rise of the New Kingdom of Egypt. The Pharoah Tutmosis I pushed southward through Kush and established frontiers between the fourth and fifth cataracts. Between 1500 and 800 B.C., the greater part of Nubia consisted of provinces which paid tribute to Egypt. Within that region, Egyptian rule over what was to become Merotic territory lasted for some 15 centuries.

The emergence of a distinctive Kushite political entity is really two sides of the same coin. One side begins with the rise to power of Napata sometime around the year 750 B.C. This development was based on Kush's control of the gold sources of Nubia.

The second thrust forward coincided with the migration from Napata to Meroÿ, nearly 200 miles southward. It was from this highly Egyptianized society that the first distinctively Kushite dynasty, corresponding to the 25th Egyptian dynasty, arose.

The Kushite rulers, who are thought to have been Libyan, took advantage of the weakness of the New Kingdom of Egypt, already in decline. They conspired with the powerful priests of the holy city of Amen-Res at Barkal to conquer Egypt.

According to the sole documentation, etched on a granite stele at the sacred mound of Jebel Barkal, the first conquest of Egypt was begun by a Kushite king called Kashta. He ruled over the country as far north as Thebes, the capital of Upper Egypt. The conquest was completed in about 731 B.C. by his son and successor, Piankhi, then in the 21st year of his reign.

Piankhi's newly acquired lands, stretching from the shores of the Mediterranean to modern Ethiopia, encompassed about a quarter of the African continent. As king, Piankhi wore the double crown, signifying sovereignty over Upper and Lower Egypt. His brother Shabako (716-695 B.C.) is said to have added to the acquisitions.

But later in the seventh century, Piankhi's son, the Pharoah Taharqa, was bested by the Assyrians, whose invading army proved to be better equipped; the Assyrians' iron weapons were superior to the bronze armament of their Kushite victims. When the Assyrians sacked Napata, the capital of Kush, the downward curve of the Kushites had begun.

Pressed by their enemies and perhaps by the deterioration of agricultural land, the Kushites began their gradual migration southward. It took the royal family 200 years to complete the move from Napata to Meroë. Still, the "new" domain was not entirely unfamiliar to them. There had always been a branch of the royal family in residence at Meroë; in fact, the city as such had been occupied for centuries.

Although the ancient Greeks knew of Meroë's existence, they confused its people with the Ethiopians. Herodotus heard of Meroë while traveling in Upper Egypt early in the fifth century. His profound interest in Egypt extended to the area in which the Kushites lived. In fact, he wrote an entire book on the Nile Valley.

Herodotus believed that Greek culture had borrowed heavily from that part of the world, especially in the field of religion. He also was convinced that sub-Saharan Africa's influence on Egypt was wide and deep. Commenting on the cultural exchange which he detected throughout the region, Herodotus wisely wrote: "I should not like to say which learned from the other."

In another observation recorded in his "Histories," Herodotus said: "The inhabitants worship Zeus and Dionysus alone of the gods, holding them in great honor. There is an oracle of Zeus there, and they make war according to its pronouncements, taking from it both the occasion and the object of their expeditions."

Unfortunately, Herodotus visited Egypt only as far south as the town of Elephantine, the site of the present-day Aswan, so we have precious little first-hand knowledge from him about Meroë.

Also, he mistakenly records in his notes that Elephantine was on the frontier between Ethiopia and Egypt when, instead of "Ethiopia," he meant the Meroitic state.

Four hundred years later Diodorus Siculus (Book I, section 32 ff.), describing the course of the Nile, mentioned in passing that the river had various islands, including Meroë. Washed as it was by its three rivers, it was sometimes mistaken for an island and so called.

Strabo collected information about Egypt and Ethiopia for his "Geography" when he was in Egypt from 25 to 19 B.C. And while interested primarily in geographical phenomena, he nonetheless left some of the most valuable data to have come down to us about the "classical past," as we shall see later.

Pliny, whose interest was in military matters, and Seneca, who sought the source of the Nile, demonstrated that the Meroitic Empire was of recognized importance to the Romans at least as late as the second century A.D. Also, there is a diplomatic record of Meroitic emissaries to Rome inscribed in graffiti at Dodecashoenos, not far from Philae south of the first cataract. Strabo also bears testimony to the empire's external relations in his account of the mission which Augustus of Samos sent to Meroë after its defeat.

The only biblical allusion which has been linked to Meroë occurs in the New Testament where, in the Acts of the Apostles (viii, 26-39), the story is told of how Philip baptized "a man of the Ethiopians." Some scholars contend the convert was a subject of Meroë and cite the passage as an indication of how widespread the knowledge of the Meroitic culture was in the early Christian centuries.

For hundreds of years thereafter, ignorance or disinterest led to almost total neglect of this area of historical investigation.

The kingdom was slumbering deep in obscurity when, in the late 18th century, the English explorer James Bruce recalled that he had passed through Meroë and casually noted " . . . heaps of broken pedestals and obelisks." Burckhardt also traveled through Meroë on his way from Damer to Shendi in April, 1814, but did not recognize the significance of the ancient site.

"I was in the company of a caravan," he wrote later, "and had the wonders of Thebes been placed on the road, I should not have been able to examine them."

The next visitors to the area came from the Sudan in 1820 --a Turco-Egyptian army sent by Mohammed Ali, the viceroy of Egypt. The army was under the command of the viceroy's son, Ismail. Frenchmen traveling with the expedition left accounts of the antiquities of the ancient sites.

The following year, two French explorers ranged through the region. Linat de Bellefonds was the first European to visit Musawwarat es Sofra, an archaeologically significant site near Meroë. More importantly, he visited the village of Begarawiya --later to be identified as the site on which the capital city of Meroë had stood. Although his work is less well known than some other 19th century explorers of the Meroë region, Linat de Bellefonds made drawings of pyramids and reliefs of the funerary chapels attached to them.

But it was the Frenchman, Calliaud, who also traveled through the region in 1821, who is credited with drawing the archaeological world's attention to the Meroë pyramids through his book published in 1826.

In 1834, Ferlini, an Italian doctor and Egyptologist, carried out his own excavations. If his account is to be believed, he removed a remarkable haul of jewels from burial sites. From 1842 to 1844, a Royal Prussian Expedition led by Lepsius recorded a large number of monuments. As a scholar alert to the area's significance and its relationship to Egyptian history, Lepsius made a particularly heavy contribution in his works to the body of Meroitic archaeological knowledge.

But it remained for the German archaeologist, Garstang, in 1911, to definitively establish the location of the capital of classical Meroë as being at Begarawiya, the same village visited nearly a century earlier by Linat de Bellefonds.

Even after the rediscovery, it was difficult to trace the plan of the ancient city. Many of the structures were in pitifully ruined condition or had vanished altogether because the perishable materials of which they had been built had yielded to destruction by time and perhaps fire. One noteworthy artifact that survived was a massive, 15-ton sarcophagus with a 4-ton lid.

The region's natural features and the local circumstances could easily have provided the former Kingdom of Kush with the base to transform itself into the prototype industrial Empire of Meroë. The landscape that Pliny described in his "Natural History" gives a picture of the setting: "In the vicinity of Meroë, greener herbage begins. A certain amount of forest comes into view. The tracks of rhinoceros and elephant can be seen."

Although the entire area of Meroë is called Butana, Dr. Hintze, one of the first archaeologists to work there, says this is merely a simplified designation. Actually, he says, only the pasture land was called Butana.

In any case, the extensive, grassy Butana plains from which hills rise to a considerable height is the locale of Meroë. The city of Khartoum now stands at the edge of the desert. But at the beginning of the historical period, the southern limits of the desert were to the north, nearer to the Egyptian frontier.

Encompassing a broad swath of the Nile's east bank, Meroë's capital was the residence of kings from the sixth century B.C. to the end of the fourth century A.D. To the east, temples and cemeteries stretched out on the plain overlooked by low hills on which stand the burial pyramids of the ancient rulers. Much of the area is unexcavated.

The unexcavated section contains, among other things, mounds of iron slag. To the untutored eye, they are nothing. Yet it was on iron that much of Meroë's political, economic and cultural eminence was based. Therefore, the slag heaps, though still incompletely studied, are of the highest archaeological importance.

Iron was readily accessible in the Meroë region. It lay atop the sandstone of the Nubian plains. A surface crust of ferricretes, a phenomenon caused by the movement of underground iron to the surface by moisture action, is found in layers several inches thick. These mineral occurrences have the appearance of large blocks marked with a peculiar surface of glistening black nodules.

The ore was smelted in simple furnaces fired by charcoal made of wood from the acacia groves which are plentiful about the Nile.

The coming of iron to sub-Saharan Africa wrought immense changes in the social and political ideas of the people. It led to a rise in production which, in turn, supported an increased population. Iron weapons made it possible for a centralized authority to develop. The society evolved to such an extent that eventually there was ample time for leisure and the arts.

Oddly enough, African cultural evolution skipped a stage. Most of Africa went from a predominantly stone-using economy to an iron-using one. The Bronze Age, so important a step in the development of Europe and Asia, apparently was by-passed throughout much of the continent. Northern Africa was the exception. Here, the Africans had been in touch from earliest times with the peoples of the Asian Near East, where iron had been used for a millennium before it came to the African continent.

Because they used iron weapons, which they were able to produce in quantity, Meroë's military men would have had a great advantage over any local adversary. Swords and spears were part of their arsenal. No swords have been found, but they are almost invariably depicted in the hands of royal personages carved on stone reliefs. Similarly, bows and arrows appear on the stone records but so far have eluded modern excavators.

The variety of uses to which iron was put shows that it must have been smelted both day and night. The number of slag heaps that surround the capital point to a furious production. One such slag heap was used as the base of a temple.

One of the mounds of slag is traversed by a railroad cut today. During construction, fragments of a smelting furnace were discovered. The fragments indicated that the ancient furnaces were not markedly different from the clay ovens now used by a people called the Jur, who live along the River Jur in the Bahr el-Ghazal area in the Meroë region. Although the Jur do not practice the craft today, they were once famous for ironwork.

It seems apparent that Meroites fully appreciated iron, both for its practical and spiritual values. An iron arrowhead found in the tomb of Taharqa must have been regarded as particularly valuable; it was wrapped in gold leaf. Another arrowhead was found embedded between the shoulder blades of a skeleton radiocarbon dated 25 B.C.

The earliest reported discovery of iron at Meroë dates from the bitterly contested Ferlini treasure. Although Ferlini has never been considered a reliable source, it was alleged that the loot was found in the pyramid of Queen Amanshakete (45-15 B.C.). Included in the cache were a pair of shears, a broken chisel, three spoons and three needles--all of iron. Many objects were strictly for cosmetic use.

Interestingly enough, the manufacture of iron arrowheads seems to have increased until the second and third centuries and then to have ceased for a time. Later, they reappeared; and by the fourth century, judging from archaeological evidence, iron arrowheads were common.

In the same period, hoes and other agricultural implements also began to show up in considerable numbers. These tools may have served a double purpose: for domestic use and as items of trade. There are no details about Meroë's trade with Egypt, but it is reasonable to suppose that there was a considerable exchange between the neighboring peoples.

Thus, aside from its military value, iron clearly marked the path to a fuller and richer life. In the Christian era, its use increased. As we shall see in a later chapter, the Bantu people are said to have been the carriers of this knowledge to other parts of Africa in the early Christian centuries.

Iron-making was thought to have been a royal or perhaps a priestly monopoly. The kings no doubt maintained their rule through their knowledge of ironworking. In fact, they could be expected to keep the smelting process a closely guarded secret as a matter of "national security," considering the far-reaching significance of its use. In order to safeguard their monopoly, they concocted a concept of impurity and uncleanliness associated with iron-making. This concept took root and embedded itself so deeply that it is reflected in the beliefs surrounding iron which many African tribes hold to this day.

It is highly conceivable that intuition and native genius could have prompted early peoples to make use of local ore and reinvent iron smelting independently and in isolation in their own time and place. Certainly, in the opinion of the majority of Africanists, such a development did take place in Meroë. That view is consistent with the theory that there was a slow penetration southward from the Upper Nile in the first century A.D.

Among scholars committed to Meroë as the point from which iron diffused throughout sub-Saharan Africa, there is a strong supposition that Meroites, already familiar with bronze metallurgy and the kiln-firing of faience, thought through the iron-making process and so made this remarkable technological breakthrough on their own.

But other authorities have concluded that the knowledge of ironworking was brought ready-made to the Kushites and thence to the Meroites from elsewhere, perhaps from the north. This school of thought contends that the knowledge of iron-smelting was diffused southward into Nubia by Egyptian craftsmen, who in turn had learned the secret from some other source, possibly Asia.

Professor Posnansky, for one, challenges Meroë's claim as the center of iron diffusion. He argues that seafarers from India were active from early times and, through trade contacts, could have passed their knowledge of iron-making along to Africa. He further suggests that the technology first reached Africa along the Mozambique coast.

One thing is certain: however and whenever ironworking reached Meroë, its coming wrought immense changes in the community's economic, social and political life.

Stone and copper artifacts were found in even larger quantities than iron pieces. No one knows the source of copper ingots discovered at Meroë. It is thought that they must have come from Egypt, since there are no known copper deposits in the Meroë area. Conversely, the Egyptians had produced copper objects for many centuries but apparently were not interested in mastering the skills of obtaining iron and then working it. In fact, the Egyptians prized iron as a rarity. Otherwise, they were content to use bronze. The people of Meroë were far faster in making use of iron.

There are differing opinions on the origins of divine kingship. One associates it with iron technology, as we have seen.

But others reject the hypothesis that iron technology was necessary to give impetus to conquest and state-building or that only a people with this capability was able to create state organization. They argue that the presence or absence of a profitable economy or the presence or absence of long-distance trade are other important factors which may have contributed to the same end. Also, this school of thought contends, development is deeply affected by the human element--clan and tribal political ambitions and other things which cannot be excavated from the ground.

Meroë probably was a monarchal state with a divine king. However, as in Egypt, Queens (Candace) played a prominent role from time to time throughout its history. In fact, one of the earliest Meroitic inscriptions, in the temple at Naqa, is by Queen Shanakdakhete.

The word "Candace," woven into the fabric of Meroitic royalty, may have corresponded to the term, "queen mother." But it is also speculated that it was the name of the queen who occupied the throne at the time of the Roman invasion. This does not suggest that queens necessarily ruled exclusively, although there are some inconsistencies on the point which archaeological detective work is only now beginning to piece together. However, one fact about the monarchy seems fairly well established: the average reign lasted for about 15 years, a time span corresponding to the average length of rule for any one person in Africa.

Excavations at Napata, the original home of the Meroitic royal family, show that its members had lived there for some time. It is also clear that the monarchs were rich and powerful.

These facts argue for an old and continuing royal line, for such a stage of development is not achieved quickly.

While the economic importance of Meroë was increasing, Napata was declining and slowly being cut off from Egypt. Gradually, the kings spent more time at Meroë. Eventually, it became their main place of residence, and they chose their queens not only from the Napatan royal family but from the aristocracy of Meroë.

Because of the absence of decipherable written records or other historical documentation, the past must be pieced together through the interpretations of archaeological finds. For the moment, the bulk of evidence about Meroë comes from the royal tombs, as has been the case in Egypt. The residences of kings are rarely found in Meroë, owing to their having been build of such ephemeral materials as wood and grass. By contrast, the royal tombs were constructed for eternity.

The birth of the Meroitic culture appears to have coincided with a historical period of relative peace and well-being. Fortifications were found, but most seem never to have been put to the test of warfare. Apparently the people of that day were not plagued by foes. Rather, they appear to have been highly skilled in the craft of peace.

In the desert at Musawwarat es Sofra were found palaces and temples which could only be identified as what we know as leisure-time abodes. One striking piece of evidence for this theory is that there are no signs of burials there. The complex must have been something of a vacation spot--what the archaeologist Crowfoot called "the superfluous works of a dynasty great in peace and prosperity."

Our knowledge of the common people of the day is scanty. The burial pyramids raised to the royal families were not their lot; hence, we have no picture of their daily lives.

Such structural remnants as have survived show that the houses were walled with blocks or slabs of sandstone or with baked red brick. At times, the bricks were covered with a fine quality of white stucco.

Probably, as Strabo recounts of the Nilotic peoples to the

north, the Meroitic plebeian class used millet as the staff of life and brewed a beer called "marise"--as those of the region do today.

The pyramids of Meroë were smaller and more sharply pointed than those of the Egyptians. Archaeological detection shows that the stonemasons marked each building block, possibly to enable the overseers to tell how work had been done by each team.

A single complex at Meroë includes 41 pyramids, the tombs of 35 kings, five queens, and two crown princes.

Such pyramids also have yielded such personal effects as royal clothing and jewelry, remnants of a regal raiment that is truly an African delight. Among these treasures are necklaces (some clearly showing Roman-Egyptian influence), pendants, armlets, bracelets, rings and earrings. We also know from these finery caches that the princes of the day dressed in flowered tunics decorated with crosses. And from cosmetic implements excavated, one can with just a little imagination picture a queen using tiny metal rods to apply antimony as eye makeup.

Interestingly enough, a fistful of pottery fragments can help to reveal the cultural growth or degeneration of a people. Meroë's classical-period pottery has been found to be decorated with elaborate friezes. Common motifs were the lotus flower and stylized ostriches and crocodiles. The level of skill of the master masons and sculptors who enhanced and illuminated the Meroitic reigns can be traced from tomb to tomb. For example, a craftsman's death can be determined by a different style or level of artistry in the works that succeed his. For the most part, the later generations of craft samples after the classical period are progressively inferior.

Pottery which had ceased to be produced in the Nile Valley a thousand years ago is still made in the Nubian Hills, a living museum of ancient arts and crafts. This is an example of "living archaeology."

Under its own impetus and through its own inspiration, Meroë invented a distinctive alphabet. It is sometimes referred to as Meroitic cursive; but this is thought to be an inaccurate term, since the characters are not connected.

Despite the distinctiveness of its alphabet, however, the Meroitic language is believed to be of African derivation--a theory which has prompted linguists to search for links with the African languages spoken today. The Meroitic language, like that of the ancient Egyptians, is now extinct.

As it has survived in samples, writing could have been used solely by the royal and priestly classes, with a demotic language current among the common people.

Samples, including those found incised on 850 archaeological fragments, show that the writing is pictographic, resembling in that respect the hieroglyphs of ancient Egypt.

Meroitic writing, like that of the Etruscans, has the distinction of being an ancient language whose phonetic values can be read with reasonable certainty but whose meaning remains elusive. The discovery of the phonetic values was made when Lepsius found a sacred boat at Wad ben Naqa. On this boat were the royal names written in Egyptian and Meroitic. Because Egyptian was well-known to scholars, the equivalent Meroitic phonetic values could be ascertained.

The people of Meroë worshipped the whole pantheon of Egyptian gods, including Apedemak, the lion-god, to whom the Meroites built one of their two-towered temples. But gradually they began revising the Egyptian pantheon and finally evolved distinct adaptations. For example, Apedemak was peculiarly Meroitic. He is pictured on the walls of tombs in many poses and forms: on his haunches, with wings and in human form with a lion's head.

He may have been a sun god or perhaps a god of war, heret-

ical rival of Egypt's Osiris. Either of these interpretations would
fit the fact that one of Apedemak's temples at Naqa was erected
on a slag heap, for iron represented strength and also had an ancient relationship with the sky. Thus, the slag mound, dated at
sometime between 150 and 50 B.C., would be a fitting base for a
temple; a number of exquisite shrines to Apedemak have also been
found at ore-rich Naqa. The lion-god is also engraved on one of
the very few rings found at Meroë.

Roman cultural influences on Meroë made for a strong mixture, even in the art of death. For example, in a third century
A.D. Meroitic tomb (where, incidentally, the largest single piece
of Meroitic iron was found) there was discovered a lamp used in
connection with funerals. The lamp was made in Meroë. It was
constructed of a diagonal rod connecting the head of a bird with a
base from which emerges a large acanthus leaf. The bird sym-
bolizes the sun, and the leaf represents the "cosmic tree," or the
"tree of life."

This type of lamp design can be linked with a tradition of
funerary lamps from Rome through Egypt to the Far East. The
iron rod, of inestimable value to them, was used because it was
supposed to be endowed with magical properties.

Such burial objects, of course, in no way exhaust the list
of connections--including cultural, industrial and political ones--
between Meroë and contemporary empires. Through her Egyptian
connections, for example, Meroë had considerable contact with
the Roman world. Gaius Petronius, who governed as Roman pre-
fect, actually sacked Napata in 23 B.C. In his valuable account
of this confrontation, Strabo related that Gaius Petronius was off
campaigning in Arabia when the Kushites attacked Syrene and carried off a statue of Emperor Augustus which the Romans had raised
in the marketplace. Upon his return, the governor sent out a puna-
tive expedition. The Meroites lost the ensuing battle. Their queen,
Amanirenas, was defeated. Although the Meroitic inscriptions
that refer to Amanirenas have yet to be deciphered, it is thought
that they might recount the Meroitic side of the event.

During the excavations carried out in Meroë, a stone head clearly of Roman style was found under the entrance doorway to one of the palaces. The head has been identified as that of Augustus. It can be seen today in the British Museum in London.

The traditionally accepted date for the end of the Kingdom of Meroë has been A.D. 350. This date is based on an inscription of King Ezana of Axum, which is interpreted as a description of the final defeat of Meroë at the hands of the Axumite army. But more recent studies suggest that Meroë may have collapsed earlier. The late third century was a period of disengagement by the Romans. In A.D. 296, they called in the Nobatae, or Noba--a people perhaps related to the Nubians. It is thought that the Noba were the cause of the decline of Meroë and that the Meroitic people eventually were overrun by them.

That Meroë was becoming more isolated and impoverished can be seen clearly in the archaeological record. There is no pottery. There are different kinds of burials. By the close of the third century A.D., Meroë had definitely gone into eclipse as a power.

Of course, its culture continued, since nothing and no one is extinguished completely by history. In a somewhat altered form, the culture can be traced to what for convenience is now called the X-group, which lived in the north. These people are still a great X factor historically and are known principally through their royal burials at Ballana and Qostol. They occupied Lower Nibia at least as far south as Firka from the beginning of the fourth century A.D. until the introduction of Christianity in the middle of the sixth century brought about profound cultural changes.

What did those people of the later-day Meroë look like? This can only be surmised. They probably would have been an aquiline-featured, brown-skinned people with varying degrees of the Negro racial strain. In fact, this is a description of the people of today's Nubia and most of the northern Sudan. There is no reason to be-

lieve that their ancient ancestors were any different in physical
appearance.

A contributing factor to Meroë's collapse may have been the
introduction of the camel into the Sahara--whether by the Romans,
the Arabs or traders from Asia who plied the desert routes between
Upper Egypt and the Red Sea. Whatever its source, the camel
revolutionized the existence of the Saharan Bedouins. They grew
from unthreatening neighbors into a positively warlike people.
Raids by the Beja, a Bedouin people, became a serious problem.
In A.D. 289 the Beja forced the Romans to abandon their holdings
south of Aswan. The Beja thus became a factor in the demise of
Meroë.

Economics also played a hand in the dwindling prosperity
of Meroë. For one thing, there was a decline in Roman markets,
owing in part to the Roman withdrawal. Also during this time,
Axum, a commercial center in northeastern Ethiopia, became a
heavy competitor for what little trade remained.

At the height of empire, Meroë encompassed varying tribal
groups that inhabited the savanna on both sides of the Nile. There
is evidence that raids were taking place in both directions from
the seventh to the fourth centuries B.C. Strabo says that the
Nubians, whom he called "Noubai," were not subjects of the Kushites even though they lived approximately between Meroë and
Dongola, west of the Nile. Axum's King Ezana described them
as people living in towns of reeds. It is also known that these
Nubians grew wheat, produced cotton and built temples to their
gods. They had camels and also used the Nile for transport.

The Nubians, who seem to have been able to live side by
side with the Kushites, were constantly at war with neighboring
Ethiopia. In his inscriptions, Ezana records that he was inces-
sently provoked by the Nubians. Owing to this aggressive behavior by his neighbors, he marched down the Atbara River,
ravaged their towns, pursued their army for 23 days and finally
defeated it.

Ezana's campaigns took him north and south of the Atbara River. The southward expedition engulfed Meroë, and it then and there fell. Unable to recover, it seems to have vanished.

Ezana departed from the habits and customs of his neighbors by accepting Christianity as the state religion. Later, his people merged into the Amharic culture of medieval Ethiopia.

The successor kingdoms were Christian and had capitals at Khartoum and Dongola. There is little archaeological evidence to support the idea that these kingdoms had any influence west of the Nile Valley. Their historical role seems to have been solely as a barrier to Moslem penetration into sub-Saharan Africa by way of the Nile Valley. After the fall of Dongola in the 14th century, the Arabs swept westward as far as Bornu, in Nigeria, where the historical record speaks unflatteringly of their incursion. They were said to have enslaved their co-religionists, who had become Islamized from Spain.

CHAPTER 3 ARABS AND AFRICANS

"There is always something new out of Africa."
Pliny, the Elder

As Meroë languished, Axum stepped in with vigor to capture what trade remained to the dying Meroitic kingdom. Commerce in ivory, gum and spices was the goal.

Axum did not spring full-grown onto the stage of history as Meroë was declining. In fact, she had been a successful trading center from about the fifth century B.C. She emerged as a prosperous trading polity in about the first century A.D., owing to the benefits derived from the active commerce being carried out at Adulis, a northern Ethiopian port. Axum was situated in the hills behind Adulis and benefited from the prosperity of the port. She was a trade link between the interior peoples and the maritime traders of the classical world.

Imports included a wide variety of basic commodities as well as luxury items. There were cotton, glass, bronze, copper and robes. There were axes and adzes for craftsmen and swords for the warriors. Among food items were olive oil and wine; and for the king, gold and silver plates.

The bulk of exports shipped out of Adulis consisted of raw materials: ivory, rhinoceros horn, tortoise shell and gold. Slaves also were an export item.

At this time, Ptolemaic Egypt carried on extensive trade with India and the Far East and made constant use of Adulis. Because of the influence of Ptolemaic Egypt, Hellenism began to penetrate the area; and the cultural links of the Sabaeans, who originated in Oman, in Southern Arabia, were gradually modified by Greek influences. It can be seen in the excavations carried out in 1950 that an indigenous blend of cultures distinct from the others was emerging. It was at about this time that altar inscriptions began appearing in Greek or Ge'ez. Ge'ez was the language of the Axumites and the forerunner of modern Ethiopian.

Zoscales, the first of a new line of Axumite kings from whom Ezana descended, became acquainted with Greek literature and acquired a taste for it. The "Periplus", a first century A.D. sailor's logbook, describes Zoscales as "miserly in his ways and always striving for more but otherwise upright and acquainted with Greek literature."

Southwest Arabia has played a leading role in the history of Ethiopia since the first millennium B.C. The Arabians were eager to expand an already flourishing mercantile system, which in every way compared favorably with that of the Phoenicians. By this time, Egyptian influence had waned in the southern Red Sea, where she had been active. The southern Arabian trade network, fully developed at this time, was ready to expand decisively. The Arabians felt that their organization was strong enough to guarantee the safety of their shipping. If this was so--and it seems to have been the case--it would imply dominion over not only maritime bases where they might dock but also over the caravan routes along which trade goods passed from the interior to the ports.

With this kind of organizational experience backing them, the Arabians arrived at Massawa, on the western side of the Red Sea littoral. Upon disembarking, they noted that this land was similar to their homeland. Here they found a hot, arid, relatively narrow coastal strip leading up to the mountains which reached an altitude of more than 6,000 feet. The moonsoons brought a well-regulated rainfall beneficial to natural vegetation and agriculture. Here, cultural development was possible. With the expansion of trade heading their list of priorities, they ascended to the plateau area, where they happily found a beneficent climate which contrasted with that of the torrid lowlands. It was here on this fertile plateau that they decided to stay.

The traders subsequently became immigrants and mingled with the Kushite peoples. There is little doubt that, while making adaptations to local conditions, they reproduced in Africa the familiar type of social, political and cultural organization which they had left in Arabia.

"They were carriers of a vastly superior civilization, both material and culture," one historian writes.

The camel, of course, arrived with them. The Arabians also brought many nutritive plants, better weapons, improvements in building techniques and construction, writing and their own language. American anthropologist George Peter Murdock says that this wave of Sabaens seized a portion of the northeastern section of what is today Ethiopia and adjacent Eritrea from the Agau, or perhaps from the Awiya--an Agau remnant. These people spoke a central Kushitic tongue and, in the main, were Christians. Although there is no proof, it is asserted in the "Cosmos"--the sixth-century "Christian Topography of Cosmos Indicopleustes"--that the Axumite Empire included the east coast trade route of Adulis-Colloe-Axum and extended into the gold-bearing area of Kenya.

It was the successors of Zoscales who built at Axum in Tigre a stele, still the object of admiration, which soared 110 feet above the landscape. Scattered about the site are the remains of temples, reservoirs and dams, all attesting to Axum's high cultural attainments. Gradually, this city-state extended its rule over the northern part of the Ethiopian plateau as far south as the Tekezzay River--an area coextensive with that in which the Tigrinya-speaking people now live.

In the fourth century A.D., Monophysite Christianity was adopted as the Axumite court religion. The development came about as a result of Axum's maritime commercial contacts with the Byzantine Empire. But Christianity was not at first accepted by the common people. From all accounts, it seems to have made effective headway only by the sixth century A.D.

It was at this time that the Axumites began to flex their military muscles. They invaded southern Arabia, the land of their ancestors, which was by no means a unified empire at that time. In fact, South Arabia was made up of four states: Ma'in, Qataban, Saba and Hadhramaut. A trade route, called the Great Incense Road, crisscrossed all four states. Whichever of the four enjoyed hegemony at any given moment controlled the commerce of the day. For some time, Saba was in a pre-eminent position in southwest Arabia. Finally, in the third century A.D., a unified empire replaced the four warring states. This union lasted only until the sixth century A.D.

It was during this period--once in the fourth century and again in the sixth century--that the Axumites crossed the Red Sea and subjugated the lands of their ancestors, thus gaining control over a strategic crosspoint on the rich Indian trade route. But in the seventh century, they were driven from South Arabia by the Persians, who themselves were expelled soon afterwards by the militancy of an emerging Islam.

After these events, the Red Sea routes became unsafe for Axumite shipping; and as a consequence, the kingdom's ties with the outside world lapsed. In the later part of the seventh century, the forces of the Beja, a nomadic people, invaded the Axumite Empire and devastated the countryside.

The Beja were the earliest pastoral nomads in Africa. They appear in Egyptian history around 2700 B.C. Both Pharaonic and Ptolemaic Egypt exploited the Beja country for gold; and the Beja, in turn, staged many incursions against the Egyptians. In the sixth century A.D., the Beja accepted Christianity; but between 1150 and 1300, they converted to Islam and remain Moslems to this day. They still live in the same general region that they occupied nearly 5,000 years ago.

Isolated from the outside world by Moslem militancy and harassed by the Beja, the weakened Axumites directed their energies against the Agau of the south. Thus suddenly the Axumites, who had accepted a form of Christianity, became more militant and especially intolerant toward their neighbors.

During the Axumite period, other Semitic immigrants entered the area. They invaded southeastern Ethiopia, leaving as their modern descendants the Gurage and Harari peoples.

Jews at this time also entered significantly into the history of Ethiopia. During the Diaspora, many merchants and emigrants fled from Arabia. The most famous of their descendants are the Falasha, or "Black Jews." They settled among the Agau and converted some to Judaism. There are many theories surrounding the presence of the Falasha, who--like the Amhara of Ethiopia-- trace their origins to Judaea. The survival to this day of ancient Hebraic influences significantly affects the over-all interpretation of Ethiopian history. A spirited historical controversy surrounds the role of the Jews. The Falasha practice a religion which is a variant of Old Testament Judaism with influences of Christianity and paganism. Their Ge'ez and Amharic-speaking neighbors have identified them in their tradition as a Jewish people. The most generally accepted hypothesis is that the Falasha are descendants of the Agau who had come in contact with either Jews or Arab converts to Judaism from Yemen, where a sixth-century Jewish kingdom was said to have flourished.

From a close study of Ethiopian history and traditions, some historians suggest that the Falasha had a role in the fall of the Axumite Empire in the 10th century. Ethiopian chronicles and the records of the Alexandrian patriarchate claim that a non-Christian queen devastated the country, burned churches and nearly did away with Axum's royal family. She was supposedly the daughter of Gideon and Judith, monarchs of the Jews of Semien.

After the younger queen (also named Judith) was married, she attacked the Axumites and replaced their royal family with her own. It is said that Judith's reign lasted 40 years and that she was succeeded by five other rulers of her dynasty.

Hand-carved ivory model of an ancient steale, as found in Axum, presented to the United Nations by Haile Selassie I, Emperor of Ethiopia. *United Nations photograph*.

Zimbabwe ruins. Southern Rhodesia. United Nations photograph.

At some undetermined time, Judith's line gave way to a new dynasty of Christian kings, called the Zagwe. They were more than likely the Agau. In the year 1270, the Zagwe were replaced by Yekuno Amlak, who claimed that he was a descendant of not only the last king of Axum but of Solomon and the Queen of Sheba. From the 13th century onward, all monarchs of Ethiopia traced their descent from the Solomonic restoration of Yekuno Amlak. Early Ethiopian records support the theory that there was an independent Jewish state southwest of the Tekazzay River in the rugged terrain of the Semian Mountains. This geographically strategic site may have been a barrier to the southward expansion of Christianity.

After the fall of Axum, other dynasties took its place in northern Ethiopia. They were sometimes Agau, sometimes Semitic. In the 12th and 13th centuries, Islam penetrated into the southeastern and eastern highlands. Islam had been established on the African continent in southern Eritrea and in Somaliland. The march of Islamic influence was checked temporarily in 1270 by a strong Solomid dynasty. The Agau converted to Christianity and became so intermingled with their Semitic conquerors that, except in isolated areas, their former central Kushitic language hardly survives today.

CHAPTER **4** RHODESIA'S RUINS OF MYSTERY

"...the mystery of Zimbabwe is the mystery which
lies in the still pulsating heart of native Africa."
                              Dr. Gertrude Caton-Thompson

"Puzzling structures," says Carl Mauch, a German geologist and gold prospector, in the 1870's upon first scanning the
ruins of Zimbabwe.

The legend of King Solomon's fabled mines seemed always
to hang impenetrably about the area. In fact, Mauch thought that
he might prove the connection between the legend and the ruins
conclusively.

Another early investigator, Theodore Bent, an antiquarian,
also was strongly affected by the aura of mystery surrounding
these ruins. Bent, commissioned by the British South African
Company and the British Association for the Advancement of Science, dug extensively in the valley and on the Acropolis--the site's
two major topographic features. At that time, he deferred judg-
ment on whether the ruins on the hill were the remnants of what
had been a copy of Solomon's Temple on Mount Morah or of the
palace where the Queen of Sheba lived during her visit to Solomon.
That they were one or the other was a popular theory in Bent's time.

Zimbabwe is the most famous archaeological site on the
continent of Africa. Situated in the Fort Victoria area of the Republic of Rhodesia (Southern Rhodesia), it lies about 17 miles
southeast of the present-day town of Fort Victoria. The ruins
cover over 60 acres and are dominated by a rocky hill with a massive walling known as the Acropolis. In the valley to the south of
the hill is a series of free-standing ruins. The principal one is
the Great Enclosure, or Temple. Situated as they are at two levels, the ruins are actually two separate complexes. But they are
linked historically.

Even though the site's obscure and tantalizing history is only now being unraveled by archaeological data and the intensive interpretation of oral traditions, the fame of Zimbabwe has, unfortunately, long been sufficiently widespread to have stimulated the curious and the destructive. For generations, looters have ransacked the ruins. One was Posselt, an explorer who visited Zimbabwe in 1888. When he arrived, he found that the main gate was in a state of collapse and that the men carrying his equipment and belongings were in awe of the ruins and were very disturbed while they were forced to remain in the vicinity.

"We climbed onto the wall and walked along this until we reached the conical tower," he wrote. "The interior was covered with dense bush; tall trees towered above the undergrowth, and suspended from there were masses of 'monkey rope' by means of which we lowered ourselves and entered the ruins."

Although Posselt claimed to have "found nothing" but "silence brooding over the scene," he has been accused of ransacking the ruins. For the "nothing" that he found included several soapstone bird sculptures. These bird figures served as a protection against lightning and invariably surround the house of a headman or the witch-doctor. People in the vicinity of Zimbabwe still regard the Bateleur eagle (Terathopius ecaduatus) as a sacred bird, and much handclapping takes place whenever it appears. This eagle is heralded by its sharp, barking cry and is generally seen on the wing, soaring majestically high overhead. This bird is still plentiful in the semi-desert and bush and savanna woodlands of East Africa. The bird sculptures are said to represent the highest achievement of the Karanga people, a branch of the Shona who today occupy Southern Rhodesia and the southern half of Mozambique. The Shona, like the Thonga who live southeast of them in southern Mozambique, are a Bantu nation. Actually, "Shona" was a European designation applied to all tribes of Mashonaland. Their origin lurks somewhere in the shadow of the Congo forests from which they moved southward into Rhodesia in the first millennium A.D.

The Karanga soapstone carvings, probably symbolic, depict birds with straight backs and folded wings. Although not positively identified ornithologically, they are thought to be hawks, crowned hornbills or black eagles.

Following his visit to Zimbabwe, Mauch propounded the theory that the roughly circular building which had stood on the Acropolis was surely a copy of Sheba's palace. When he put forward his theory in a popular magazine, he so convinced the readers of its accuracy that nothing new was added to information about Zimbabwe until 1890.

At about that time, a contingent of British soldiers sent to subdue the Mashona (Shona) camped about 17 miles from the Zimbabwe ruins. They came with the deep conviction that the Shona were very savage--and very primitive. So monolithic was the British prejudice that, although they noted the grandeur of Zimbabwe, it never for a moment occurred to them that such splendid architecture could possibly be of indigenous origin. Such monumental bias helped to lend justification to the wars of colonial conquest which were later carried out against the Matabele and the Mashona, whose descendants today occupy the very same lands on which Zimbabwe's people lived.

As British settlers moved into the region in the wake of the soldiers, those deeply rooted prejudices persisted. Although there were dissenters who labeled such behavior scandalous, these prejudices at one point evolved into a "shoot-on-sight" policy. The soldiers--the first British "pioneers" in the area-- burned the huts of the local people, whom they could not believe to be the descendants of Zimbabwe's builders.

For the settlers who followed, gold was the goal; and it was easier to seize it with an easy conscience if one despised the local inhabitants. More than 100,000 gold claims were staked out by the year 1900. These claims were later found to be on the sites of ancient gold workings.

Incalculable damage was done to the ruins in 1901 when a company was founded called the Ancient Ruins Company. The company's aim was to exploit the ruins for their gold content. But operations were forced to a halt by high costs and a Ndebele rebellion. The Ndebele were part of the Nguni nation, which had occupied Natal and pushed into the Cape of Good Hope region at about the time that South Africa was discovered. In 1838, the Ndebele had established a state by conquest in Shona territory.

R.N. Hall, curator of the Ancient Ruins Company, thought that the Zimbabwe peoples were Sabaeans from southern Arabia. His theories, which created a stir among his contemporaries, became widely accepted. But in 1905, a professional archaeologist, David Randall MacIver, stepped into the controversy. He examined the ruins with a scientific eye and an unprejudiced attitude. He took note of the most lowly pieces of pottery and paid the utmost attention to the Chinese porcelain found in the midden deposits of the ruins. Finally, he pronounced unequivocally that Zimbabwe went back to medieval times and--more important--was undoubtedly of African origin.

These conclusions so infuriated many influential people that further research was curtailed. Seeing a threat to his theory of a Sabaean origin of Zimbabwe, Hall also reasserted his hypothesis and was supported by a considerable body of opinion.

But the scientific community was on MacIver's side. However, it was not until 1929 that the British Association for the Advancement of Science commissioned Dr. Gertrude Caton-Thompson to dig anew in Central Africa. Her field work was known to be impeccable, and her conclusions would therefore carry great authority. Dr. Caton-Thompson analyzed the stratigraphy and studied the African pottery along with the imported wares. She dated Zimbabwe from the eighth to the ninth centuries A.D. and placed its cultural apex in the 13th century. And as a crowning conclusion, she announced that the ruins were definitely the work of Africans.

Commenting on the significance of her findings, she said:

"The interests in Zimbabwe and allied ruins...enriches, not impoverishes, our wonderment of their remarkable achievement; it cannot detract from their inherent majesty, for the mystery of Zimbabwe is the mystery which lies in the still pulsating heart of native Africa."

Dr. Caton-Thompson was able to clear the clouds of controversy considerably by stating unequivocally that, except for a few luxury imports, every item deposited in the ruins declared itself to be of Bantu origin of medieval times. In 1958, excavations were carried out at Zimbabwe by Roger Summers, Keith Robinson and Anthony Whitty. As reported in their work, published in 1961, radiocarbon dating confirmed the settlement date suggested earlier by MacIver and Dr. Caton-Thompson.

The Zimbabwe ruins, at the head of the Mtelikwi Valley, are not themselves situated in a gold bearing area. But the region had other natural advantages: It was green the year round, owing to the rain-laden winds from the Indian Ocean and local mists. Because of these climatic conditions, Zimbabwe was favorably situated for, among other things, rainmaking ceremonies.

The top of the Acropolis is divided into a series of enclosures formed by large boulders linked by stone walling. At the western end of the hill is a large, free-standing enclosure and a small entrance. All of the enclosures were found to contain deep deposits of occupation debris, indicating long residence. These layers have yielded potshards and the valuable samples from which radiocarbon dates have been obtained.

The Temple in the valley is a great, circular enclosure with walls which average some 24 feet in height and reach a maximum thickness of 17 feet at the base. It was presumably constructed by starting at one end and lengthening the wall segment on the ramp principle, working slowly around in a circle until the two ends were joined. One part of the wall is decorated with a chevron design. The entire structure encloses earlier walls of the same type but built on a much smaller scale. Within these smaller compounds is housed a conical tower, whose purpose is wrapped in mystery. Also within the inner wall are a number of small stone enclosures as well as traces of mud huts and other indications that people lived there. Here, too, early excavators harvested gold, Chinese procelain and other precious items.

The people of the ruins were wealthy and apparently religious. The East African coastal trade was a stimulus to the inhabitants to exploit their copper and gold deposits, which were the raw materials for the commerce of the region. However, the mining was not necessarily done by those who occupied the Acropolis and valley of Zimbabwe.

For clarity, it will be useful at this point to explain what--in the context of the Zimbabwe Empire--constitutes the "Iron Age." The specialized use of the term was introduced in 1950 for the purpose of accuracy. Encompassing the past 2,000 years of history, it refers to a complex of post-Stone Age cultures in Southern Rhodesia. The cultures vary, but there is a general use of iron tools and weapons. The south-central African sequences reveal no copper- or bronze-using stage between the use of stone and iron. This is unlike the sequences in Europe and the Near East. The Bronze Age seems to have been skipped, as we have seen, in sub-Saharan Africa.

The Iron Age can be divided into two parts. First, there is the Southern Rhodesian Iron Age A, which goes from the earliest known iron-users, possibly dating from 100 B.C., up to the beginning of the 19th century. Secondly, there is the Southern Rhodesian Iron Age B, which began in about the 12th century and developed independently of A up to the beginning of the 19th century. Subsequently, the two mingled.

Iron-using and Bantu expansion seem to go hand and hand. And it was they who have diffused ironworking from Meroë.

Gradual though this expansion was, it clearly carried along with it people who knew the techniques of farming and could make use of iron for their own defense. It is said that in their movements, they released" these skills to others. By A.D. 800, they had reached the Limpopo River and moved southward to present-day South Africa. A two-pronged expansion took place in East Africa: one to the southern part of Uganda and the other to the central and western parts of Kenya and central and western Tanzania. African tradition has the Bantu moving south and southwestward from the Tana and Juba Rivers to the edge of Kenya and Somalia, but this is unreliable evidence at the moment. There were other movements and population shifts--like that of the Masai in about A.D. 1300--when cultures became differentiated.

Professor George Peter Murdock says that Uganda is closer to the original Bantu homeland than any other section of Africa. It presumably was the first place to be reached by them as they entered the periphery of the tropical forest by way of the Congo River.

This remarkable movement of peoples brought with it a pattern of despotic government practiced on a large scale. The Bantu inhabitants of the rain forest provinces did not show any high degree of political integration--probably a sign of their great wisdom, for they had no need of any elaborate political organization. As they moved, presumably they were influenced by other ideas; and as they settled, they borrowed or annexed the political patterns they had learned from others. When the Bantu pierced the forests of northern Mozambique, the Bushmen, who were resident at that time, were exterminated. There has been no trace of them found today. The Bantu entered Tanganyika (The Republic of Tanzania), no one knows whether from Uganda or the south.

Seemingly, a peaceful migration at this point turned them from migrants to invaders. It is thought that there were actually two waves of migrants--one peaceful and the other using war as a means--perhaps corresponding to the two Iron Ages. When they reached the coastal region just opposite Zanzibar, they encountered a wholly new group of people, ones that they had never encountered before. They were not Bushman hunters whom they had been displacing and intermingling with along the way but presumably the descendants of the ancient Azanians. No one knows exactly how they established themselves, but they did so solidly and became the dominant population. These estimates of time and settlement are hazy at the moment, but further research may clear up the discrepancies and sort out one of the most phenomenal population movements in the history of the African continent. The entire period covering the Bantu movements throughout Africa is loosely called that of the "Bantu migration."

The word "Bantu" in itself is a cause of confusion among Africanists. It seems to apply indiscriminately to a group of languages, a complex of cultures and a racial group. At the moment, we have no knowledge of what language the earlier metal-users of Central Africa spoke. Therefore, it is incorrect to use the word "Bantu" in reference to culture or race. For that reason, the term "Iron Age" was felt to be more precise and efficient, as we have discussed previously.

For the purposes of clear historical exposition, the occupation of Zimbabwe is divided into four essential periods. The first period is characterized by a kind of pottery labeled Gokomere pottery. Gokomere is a place located near Fort Victoria and was excavated in the 1930's. The vessels have thick walls, which indicate imperfect firing. The pottery was found in an Iron Age layer of occupation overlying a Stone Age deposit. In general, this pottery was undecorated and had a considerable variety of shapes. Spouted pottery was made there, too, but was not in general use. Gokomere pottery found at Zimbabwe at its lowest layer, or earliest occupation level, was excavated from the ocherous earth which formed an overburden to the hill's underlying rock. Eventually, the pottery traditions of the Gokomere spread widely over Rhodesia.

Although clues to the culture of the Gokomere people are few, traces from such near-by sites as Mabveni in Mashonaland affirm its presence. A storage granary built of mud and sticks and resting on a timber framework standing on four stones was one of the structures found. Partly from this discovery, it was presumed that agriculture was practiced. Although no seeds have been found, it is thought that the Gokomere's agricultural methods were conditioned by their use of simple tools with which the infertile soil was worked.

The Gokomere kept livestock, too, for the excavations have yielded sheep mandibles. They may also have herded cattle, although no remains of these animals have been found. Certainly, they hunted, for buffalo, impala, wildebeest and zebra were there for the taking. Much time was spent in the gathering of naturally occuring foods to supplement the diet provided by their domestic herds and agricultural output.

Although the Gokomere used some metal implements, metal-working seems not to have been practiced intensively. Iron fragments from Zimbabwe are rare for this period.

Paraphenalia has been found at Zimbabwe to indicate that religious rituals were performed by the Gokomere. This would not be surprising in view of the fact that ritual practices were fully developed elsewhere in the area by this time.

In the fourth century A.D., these Iron Age farmers and pottery-makers abandoned the Zimbabwe Acropolis.

The Gokomere were succeeded by the Period II occupants, whose origin is unknown. Although primarily an agricultural people, the newcomers hunted with bone- and iron-tipped arrows. They built no stone walls to mark their occupation for modern archaeologists. However, the thin-walled huts in which they lived were of a kind that still exist among the peoples of the region today. Both are constructed of poles and daga (mud plastering).

The ceramic style departed from that of the Gokomere; among other things, it was characterized by the production of stylized human figurines and strikingly realistic models of their cattle.

A different picture arises from the excavations of the Period III occupation which radiocarbon dating has established as having lasted from about A.D. 1075 to 1440. The thin-walled huts of the Period II occupants were uprooted and thrown over the side of the Acropolis. In their place, more substantial floors were built and better huts rose on them.

It is clear that a new system of building was taking place, not only with habitations but with the more monumental structures. At the Acropolis, the Period III people began construction of the south wall of stone slabs. These inhabitants specialized in building on rock formations. It was also during this period that the first structures were raised in the valley of Zimbabwe. Simultaneously, pottery-making improved. For example, the potters used finer clay and graphite and burnished their wares. Different pottery types existed side by side--an indication of the diversity of work and life that went on throughout the period.

Despite differences, the material culture of Zimbabwe during Period III shows continuity from that of the previous people. There are indications that the Period III occupants arrived in small numbers and perhaps dominated those already living there. Such innovations as were made in the later days of Period III were probably introduced by the predecessors of the present-day Shona people. There is little specific information about the extent of territory occupied by the Period III inhabitants of Zimbabwe, but they must have spread over a wide area.

Then, for some undetermined reason, a period of impoverishment set in. Huts were burned, revealing a fundamental weakness in the social structure and a lack of cultural stability. Yet judging from Acropolis deposits, Period III represented the time of the longest distinctive occupation before it lost its identity.

It was followed by Period IV--the time of greatest activity and an era of continuous architectural development in the Great Enclosure. Judging from archaeological finds, the impoverishment of Period III suddenly gave way to great richness. Glass beads, china and assorted imports have been excavated in profusion. So have ornaments of gold, iron and copper...indigenous pottery in a variety of shapes...copper ingots and tools, weapons and gongs of iron. Gongs are a symbol of authority.

The pottery was dated from 1440 to 1833, when Chief Zwangendaba's Nguni destroyed Zimbabwe. This pottery is said to be that of the Rozwi, a branch of the Shona people. The chevron design, which decorates not only the Temple wall but much of the pottery, was found to be widespread at this time and may have been connected with some of the local chieftianships.

The Rozwi arrived at Zimbabwe in A.D. 1500. During the Rozwi period, the enormous amount of stone building for which Zimbabwe is noted took place. The construction technique, characterized by the use of dry stone without mortar binding, was developed independently in the region. Zimbabwe's structures bear no relationship to the stone work of Ethiopia.

Even hut construction became an artistic work. As mentioned earlier, the foundations were especially noteworthy. At this time, objects which could only be called exotic were found, probably the result of trade and contact with foreigners. Although the relics of Rozwi workmanship are rare, the close association with copper and gold was a fact of their lives.

Historically, Zimbabwe spans the entire Rhodesian Iron Age and is considered to be a key site. The earliest ritual acts of the Iron Age must have taken place on the rocky summit of the Acropolis. These ancient practices may have been in some way connected with the cult of Mwari, part of the monotheistic Shona religion. The Eastern Enclosure must have been a religious center. The Acropolis, with its hidden passages and complex ascent, most probably was the dwelling place of the chief of the Mwari cult. The hill was probably restricted to a select few. The ordinary people must have been relegated to the valley, which was also the headquarters site for the vast organization made up of administrative lords whose center was Zimbabwe.

Having established the Zimbabwe sequence, we can now consider some of the more important phases in detail.

CHAPTER 5   A STORY IN STONE

"It is difficult to identify another association of states which can vie with the Empire of Monomotapa."

D. P. Abraham

It was during the second millennium A.D. that the Karanga peoples came to dominate the area between the Zambezi and the Limpopo Rivers. This great confederacy of peoples was ruled by chiefs who resided in splendor at Zimbabwe. By the middle of the 15th century, the Rozwi Mambos were in firm control of the Karanga nation. The territory now occupied by Southern Rhodesia forms the northwestern half of an uninterrupted area of Bantu-speaking peoples extending from the Kalahari Desert in the northwest to the shores of the Indian Ocean in the southeast and on the north by the Zambezi and on the south by the Limpopo. The southeastern part falls within Portuguese East Africa, but there was a period when the whole area constituted one socio-political continuum.

One expert, D. P. Abraham, has done much to record and interpret the oral tradition of the region. After extensive study, he concludes:

"It is difficult to identify another association of states which can vie with the Empire of Monomotapa for the length of historical development, variety of ethnic origins and impacts and complexities of problems associated with the catalytic action of not one but two communities of exotic provenance, to wit, the Arabs and the Portuguese; furthermore, the unique status of the empire for ethnohistorical research is highlighted by the impressive character of its sacro-political monuments and by the range of contemporary documentation available right through from the 16th to the early 20th century."

The Karanga, who formed the nucleus of this occupation period, entered Rhodesia south of the Zambezi from the Lake

Tanganyika area in about A.D. 850. They were familiar with
mining and quickly located the copper and gold deposits. They
fashioned ornaments from these metals and developed a more ele-
gant life style than that of their crude pastoral neighbors. Their
ancestor cult led them to establish shrines, the principal one being
called Dzimba Dzemabwe, meaning "Houses of Stone." This religious complex became the focal point of their nation and the place
in which the leader of the Rozwi people lived. They were politi-
cally clever and established an overlordship over a loose confederacy of vassal chiefs, who paid them tribute in gold dust and
ivory. Their military organization became tighter and more efficient when, in the 13th century, they came under pressure from
peoples from Bechuanaland who had begun moving into their territory because the Kalahari Desert was growing increasingly arid
and uninhabitable.

In 1425, Mutota, the Rozwi king at Monomotapa, under-
took a campaign of conquest of the plateau area. He later drove
successfully toward Mozambique on the East African coast.

The name "Monomotapa" is actually a Portuguese distor-
tion of a local title, Mwanamutapa, meaning "Lord of the Plun-
dered Lands." As new arrivals, the Rozwi employed the local
population as ironworkers and cattle-herders. The latter were
a relatively evolved people who were themselves familiar with
cattle-breeding, hoe agriculture and masonry.

The term "Rozwi" did not become current until the 17th
century. It was applied to a ruling clan of the Karanga nation who
rose to power through political acumen. The Rozwi remained
aloof from the common people and received produce, cattle and
trade materials as tribute. They also traded with their northern
neighbors. Interestingly, the fact that gongs were included in this
commerce suggests that this symbol of power and authority made
its way from the Congo and was adopted by the Rozwi.

Around 1440, the Rozwi king headed a military campaign
to secure for himself the lands of southern Africa bounded by the

Indian Ocena, the Limpopo, the Zambezi and the Kalahari Desert. Because economic activity had reached a fever pitch in the Mono-motapa-Zimbabwe area, overpopulation was becoming a problem and territorial expansion a necessity. Salt supplies, absolutely essential for human survival, also were becoming scarce. King Mutota's energetic leadership fostered successful campaigns in the area of present-day Rhodesia. He reached the eastern borders by 1450. The Arab traders followed in the path of his successful campaigns and established trading posts. It was as a result of Mutota's military victories that his victims gave him the name Mwene Mutapa, meaning "master pillager."

The pattern of conquest was followed in the next 30 years by his son, Mutope, who added to the already sprawling domain. Mutope kept this kingdom together by a system of vassalage. The political links and especially the lines of communication were not strong throughout these vast lands. The usual political intrigues, fired by cultural differences, led to a rapid disintegration. Eventually, the empire broke down into its component parts, separated from any central authority. Changa, a Rozwi vassal in charge of the southern part of Monomotapa, began to regard himself as a king and styled himself to fit the part of an independent ruler. When Mutope died in 1480, Changa took the opportunity to flout the authority of Mutope's successor, Nyahauma. Changa changed his name to Changamire at this time. So ambitious did he become that le led a military campaign in which he conquered Nyahauma in a battle in 1490. For about four years, he ruled as Changamire I over all the Rozwi territories. Then, a comeback was staged by Nyahauma's son, Kakuyo Komunyaka, who killed Changamire. As a result of tactically clever moves, Kakuyo Komunyaka not only regained his father's lands but asserted authority over all the eastern and southeastern parts.

The beliefs of the people of Monomotapa were intimately connected with their method of political organization. They followed a complex kind of ancestral cult with a diety of great importance at the apex. The spirits of ancestors provided a means of communication with the supreme being. Both the Shona and Rozwi Empires were profoundly influenced by these beliefs. Both believed in a supreme being as the creator of the world of man.

The Shona divinity goes under different names; the most commonly used is Mwari, which might come from the term "Muri," meaning "you are." Intermediaries must intercede with Mwari; no living man can do so. Spirit worship has evolved among the Shona people because they believe that a man can speak with the Creator after death. When someone wants a favor or seeks protection from the Mwari, the supplicant prays through his own ancestral spirits. These spirits, known as mbondoro (the tribal spirits) are the means by which the whole community or its representatives can intercede with the Mwari in times of stress. The comparable family spirit is called the vadzimu. Much of the people's lives is concerned with this worship.

Both the mbondoro and the vadzimu are thought to express themselves through a medium, called svikiro. The host may be a member of a family to whom the vadzimu belongs or, in the case of the community as a whole, any member may act as host. For purely practical reasons, there is extreme respect for the elders in this cult. Since communication can only be made with the Mwari by way of ancestral spirits, the Shona wisely show considerable respect for the tribal elders and the older family members.

The powers of the Shona and Rozwi chiefs were based on their intermediary role. The king presided over a highly organized court system. There were a chancellor, court chamberlain, military commander, keeper of the sacred tribal relics, head drummer, head cook, head doorkeeper and many other specialized functionaries. These titles were passed on from one office-holder to another. There were also a queen mother and nine official wives. Each was said to have had her own small court and officials attached to it within the official enclosure. There also were thought to have been some 3,000 serving people, mostly women. Away from the court, governors and other representatives of the king were in authority. They, too, were said to live in a grand manner. The king's officials were expected to send their sons to the Monomotapa court at Zimbabwe so that they might become pages or warriors in the monarch's service.

A reaffirmation of allegiance to the king was a very important annual ceremony. Every May, the ruler's subjects would come and light their own fires from the royal fires. This was to symbolize the rekindling of allegiance. When the king died, the fire was extinguished until a new monarch took his place.

It is abundantly clear that Monomotapa's monarch was not just a ruler in the ordinary sense. He also exercised divine kingship, a concept that is common throughout Africa. His subjects must only approach him in the most servile manner--on their stomachs. They were not allowed to look at him. They would be privileged to listen to his voice emerging from behind a curtain or screen. The king's acts during such an audience were imitated by those present. For instance, if the king coughed, everyone would do so.

It was essential that, to his subjects, the king must always appear to be in excellent health; for it was believed that any disability which the ruler might suffer would endanger the health of the entire state. Illness or old age could be an ugly drama. The king must, if the well-being of the kingdom was endangered through his own infirmity, take poison so that a younger and more vigorous man might replace him and assume his duties. Upon the king's death, it was thought that his spirit entered that of a lion. The lion subsequently was a revered and even sacred animal who could not be killed except at a hunt in the presence of the ruling monarch. The attributes of the lion were frequently used in reference to the king.

When the Portuguese arrived on the East African coast at Kenya in about 1505, they found Komunyaka was in effective control of the northern half of Rhodesia along with a strip of country about 200 miles wide running east and southeast to the Indian Ocean. The log book of Vasco da Gama, chronicling his passage up Africa's East Coast from the Cape of Good Hope and on across the Indian Ocean in 1488-89, records his astonishment and that of his crew when they discovered the civilization and prosperity of the East Coast.

Although we are not here concerned with details of the Portuguese dismemberment of first the sovereignty of Monomotapa and then its land, a brief mention might be useful to round out Monomotapa's history.

In 1515, Antonio Fernandes, a pardoned criminal, became the first of the Portuguese explorers to penetrate Monomotapa. No one can say what routes he took, but it is thought that he followed those of Arab traders, which would have been the sensible thing to do. He may have visited the gold mining districts of Mashonaland, the Mazoe Valley and the Lomagundi district. Zimbabwe was not on his itinery, but he seems to have spoken with a person of authority from Monomotapa. Apparently, it was a friendly discussion.

As a result of Fernandes' pioneering efforts and his reports from the interior, the Portuguese slowly but surely developed a pattern of trading relations with Monomotapa. By the 16th century, commercial control of the interior seems to have been firmly in Portugal's grip. But Lisbon's policy caused tension which led to a bitter battle in which the Africans attempted to drive out the Portuguese. In some cases, the Portuguese made local compacts with the chiefs and developed a puppet regime; and eventually they had to recognize the ascendancy of one or more leaders in the region in order to carry out their program of economic exploitation. These political events and their effects must have been a turning point in the lives of the indigenous people. But nothing about this aspect of events is revealed in the documentary records of the Portuguese or in the oral tradition of the Karanga people.

The Portuguese believed--and rightly--that the gold whose entrepot was coastal Kilwa was mined in the neighboring regions around Monomotapa. The central plateau is marked with ancient workings even now. The zone from the surface to 20 feet down was said to be very rich in gold. Much of it was carried away by Portuguese traders; but in comparison to what existed, they got very little, for they were not trusted in the interior.

There is little doubt that the Swahili port city of Kilwa had as much influence on the interior's development as the inland mineral wealth had on Kilwa, which prospered as a result. A Portuguese royal agent in 1512 and 1515 reported that through Sofala (Mozambique) the annual average gold shipment was about 100 pounds. He also reported that larger quantities of ivory, copper, amber, seed pearls, coral and a few slaves were traded. Apparently, slaving was of little interest at the time.

The Portuguese were fully aware of the value of the inland country. They tried by every means to garner the benefits of the interior, but the Swahili merchants were far from communicative. In 1573, the king of Monomotapa ceded to the Portuguese a large area between the Sena and Tete Rivers. Gradually, the Europeans moved in and cleared plantation sites, at the same time using political and military strategems to gain their colonial ends. Interestingly enough, the Rozwi Empire held its own in the southern region despite the Portuguese incursions.

There were other kings who ruled in the upland region on the frontier of Southern Rhodesia and Portuguese East Africa. At this time, the power of the Monomotapa's monarch was limited to the northeastern districts and the northwesterly fringe of Mozambique. The Rozwi in the more southerly regions built and embellished the walls of Great Zimbabwe, raising them higher and higher as they went. The empire lasted for 200 years before it was invaded by other Africans.

In 1607, Monomotapa experienced an internal revolt. The king's vassals were rebelling. He called in the Portuguese for help; and they came, led by Diogo Simoes. But their assistance cost Monomotapa dearly. After Simoes proved victorious, he persuaded the emperor to part with all the gold mines. In an agreement of August, 1607, the Monomotapa ruler did "think fit and am pleased to give his Majesty all the mines of gold, copper, iron, lead and pewter which may be in my empire, as long as the King of Portugal, to whom I give the said mines, shall maintain my position."

But within two decades, Portuguese intervention was meeting active resistance. Portuguese records of the period show that the Monomotapa emperor and his forces killed the ambassador which the Portuguese captain at Mozambique had sent to him. The African's forces fought the Portuguese for two years but were defeated. Apparently, Monomotapan independence was completely destroyed during this period. The Portuguese managed to maneuver into place a puppet ruller who seems to have converted to Christianity. A treaty was finally signed with the Portuguese in May 24, 1629, providing that "throughout all his kingdom he shall allow as many mines to be sought for and opened as the Portuguese like."

Rozwi history does not end here. The Khami ruins near Bulawaya, in southwestern Rhodesia, have been identified as the cultural heir to the Zimbabwe peoples. In fact, Khami was a Karanga state. It was built in 1700 and occupied for about 100 years.

In the spirit of Zimbabwe, the focal point of the Khami site is the hill ruin. All the visible buildings now reveal that the idea of a raised platform supporting huts of daga, wood and thatch existed there. Livestock enclosures bounded by free-standing walls also were a construction feature noted by modern archaeologists. Though unlike those at Zimbabwe, these enclosures nevertheless were skillfully constructed. Blocks of granite were used for the walling. Chevron and checkerboard patterns were engraved on the blocks.

A hut used for ceremonies, or perhaps as a repository for relics, has been deduced from one ruin--apparently the remains of a structure destroyed by fire. China and stoneware salvaged from the site date from the late 16th century to the early 17th century. Carved ivory objects also have been excavated. It is speculated that the ivory objects, discovered in the ceremonial hut ruins, were left behind only because of a sudden raid that forced the occupants to flee in a hurry. The china and stoneware finds were so meagre as to suggest that much had been carried off by Portuguese looters. What little gold has been found includes beads thought to have been collected in tribute extracted by the Mambos of Khami from their mining neighbors. Ironworking was known in the region, although it seems not to have been practiced on a large scale.

At least superficially, foreign influences gradually began to transform these descendants of the people of Zimbabwe. The foreign invasion of ideas and objects merely changed some of the details of their material culture without significantly affecting the basic structure. Their fundamental pattern of social organization remained the same throughout the centuries.

Why did they survive so long? Perhaps their closely knit social organization is the answer; more specifically, it may have been that the close religious ties between the king and the spiritual head of the Mwari cult led to a certain kind of conservatism in their customs and culture militating against change.

Today the Shona--or Mashona, as they are sometimes called--occupy a culturally homogeneous nation of more than a million inhabitants who live in Southern Rhodesia and the Portuguese colony of Mozambique.

CHAPTER 6 PEOPLE OF THE HILLS

Along the eastern border of Rhodesia, deep in the heart of the Inyanga Mountains, lies a 3,000-square-mile region which has been described as "one vast ruin field." Cairns and monoliths in profusion mark the landscape.

The earliest travelers who followed Cecil Rhodes to the area were profoundly impressed by the ruins scattered over what is called the Inyanga Escarpment, even though they were unable to identify what they saw. Since then, archaeological investigation has cast some light on the subject, but much still remains in the dark. Enough is known, however, to realize that among these hills are the material clues that attest to the last great southward Bantu movement to affect Southern Rhodesia. It was here that an act in the history of the Rhodesian Iron Age was played out; and certainly the story of Inyanga's inhabitants was linked inextricably to that of their Shona neighbors.

For convenience, the region of occupation may be divided into two topographic levels: the uplands rising above 5,000 feet and the lowlands below that altitude.

The vanished dwellers of Inyanga belonged to related tribes. Those of the uplands, which were occupied in the 15th and 16th centuries, were of Shona stock and were responsible for the stonework, for which they were also famous at Zimbabwe.

The most striking characteristic of this vast collection of ruins is the splendid example of contoured terracing walled in by stonework. It is still uncertain whether the terraces were cultivated; for although similar ones appear at Zimbabwe, they were in no way connected with agriculture. On the other hand, terracing was a normal method of cultivating hill country in many parts of the world. Rice in China and tea in India and Ceylon are grown on these great hillside steps even today. Evidence of terrace cultivation also has been found in Africa: in Tanganyika, in the Transvaal and in parts of the continent's central and northern regions.

But the terracing at Inyanga appears to have been developed--or perhaps reinvented--independently. The stair-step ruins of the Inyanga dwellers are wholly unconnected with similar "landscaping" elsewhere in Africa.

Why these terraces? There is a theory that the people occupied the infertile mountains because they were forced to. Having once known--but forgotten--the technology of terracing for cultivation, they were obliged by the necessity of survival to reinvent hillside engineering. This theory, of course, attributes an agricultural function to the terracing. The hypothesis gains support from the discovery that the Inyanga terraces are crossed by furrows built for irrigation and drainage purposes and may extend for miles from a constant water source--perhaps ever-flowing springs or streams.

In other Inyanga structures, too, a gradual evolution in building took place. One of the site's major features is its stone-lined pits, to be found at about the 5,000-foot altitude. Part of each pit was excavated out of the hillside, and the remainder is surrounded by a wall. Local tradition says that they were used as enclosures for calves and other small livestock. Driven into the pit at nightfall, the animals could be sealed in and kept safe from prowling predators by passing stout sticks across the entry-way.

Another architectural feature of the ruins is the complex of strongly constructed forts which stand sentry about the slopes of the Inyanga Mountains, which form part of the chain of high peaks that border the African plateau all the way from the Cape of Good Hope to Ethiopia.

All indications point to an occupation by the terrace builders from the 16th to the 18th centuries.

As for the Inganga generally, the supposition is that theirs was an impoverished culture, remote from the mainstream of African development and unnourished by the richness and sophistication of some of their neighbors.

For example, the pottery--whose tradition was transmitted from mother to daughter--is of a lower standard than the rich craftsmanship of Zimbabwe and considerably below that of the Ziwa who occupied the Inyanga region from early in the first millennium to A.D. 1050. A kind of "ribbed pottery" was found at Inyanga, much like that of the Zimbabwe ruins and similar to ribbed shards recovered from Gedi, a city-state on the coast of Kenya. Professor Kirkman ventures to identify the Gedi shards as ancestral to the Rhodesian ribbed ware. He dates his finds at the 12th century A.D. Kirkman says that the style was introduced into the Rhodesian gold-mining area by the coastal peoples who acted as middlemen between the Arab traders of the coast and the miners of the interior.

As for ironwork, the Inyanga ruins yielded only simple objects: arrowheads, some barbs and the keys of hand pianos--a primitive instrument composed of metal vibrators and resonator.

Aside from the domesticated animals hypothesized from the stone-lined pits, the Inyanga hunted game for food. They also cultivated sorghum, millet, maize and groundnuts (peanuts)--crops which do not require great soil fertility and which are grown in Rhodesia today.

There is a suggestion that the Inyanga Mountain region was settled by immigrants from the north who came from the hilly country of southern Malawi, where pressure by Congo Basin tribesmen forced the population to move.

Although it is speculated that Inyanga's upland forts were built in response to 16th century Zimba invasions--military intrusions depicted in the Portuguese records--, occupation by the Inyanga appears to have continued long afterwards. Another theory is that the terrace builders suffered at the hands of the Nguni tribes, or were at least threatened by these warlike neighbors who lived to the south.

But one thing seems certain: far from being exterminated or routed in haste by a sudden invasion, the Inyanga left every sign of having made a leisurely, orderly withdrawal to a new home- land. Indeed, this conclusion is supported by the very scarcity of the archaeological evidence of occupation. Evidence shows that when a kraal (the often stockaded village unit of South Africa) has been overrun and sacked, it yields a wealth of artifacts left behind as useless by the belligerents but often invaluable to archaeologists. At Inyanga, the withdrawal apparently was made under other cir- cumstances. The evidence indicates that the site was thoroughly stripped by its occupants in preparation for a perhaps forced but nevertheless unhurried migration. It may have been that they felt obliged to ally themselves with one of their powerful neighbors and so abandoned their terraced fields. Further investigation may yet clarify whether their migration was due to economic or military pressures of the moment.

MAPUNGUBWE

Although populated and ruled by different immigrants, the southern plateau of Rhodesia exhibits a continuity of human settle- ment. One of the most spectacular archaeological sites in the region is Mapungubwe, which translates as "Place of the Jackals." These ruins are situated on a 1,000-foot-long, flat-topped butte, or mesa, whose precipitous cliffs rise 100 feet above the low hills and the Limpopo River flood plains. The site lies to the south of the Limpopo and Shashi Rivers and on the border between the present-day states of South Africa and Southern Rhodesia. It was excavated between 1934 and 1940.

Archaeological finds reveal that the Limpopo Valley was the southernmost province of the Shona Empire. It is one of the wildest and most desolate regions in what is called the northern Transvaal. Lions and elephants roamed about in their daily quest for food. The local peoples were absolutely certain that Mapungubwe was a sacred mount and that their ancestors, "the great one," had buried treasure on its truncated summit.

There was a tale circulating through the area--a very sparsely settled one--that a white man had gone to live in the wilds in a hermit's cave on the banks of the Limpopo. The story was true. A well-known local eccentric had set up housekeeping in this remote wilderness about half a mile from Mapungubwe. He had staked a claim to the hill, climbed to the summit and found things there. In fact, it was an earthenware pot which he presented to someone who, in turn, told a white farmer named Van Graans that touched off the initial adventure that led to scientific investigation.

The story of Mapungubwe's discovery is one dear to the hearts of most adventurers. Nothing was known about the mysterious mesa except that the Africans who lived in the region considered it a fearful place--too fearful even to discuss. When they were forced to pass within sight of Mapungubwe, they kept their backs turned to it and their eyes averted. Certainly they refused to climb it, for they felt that if they did they would surely be doomed. To this day, the Venda people who live in the region are still terrified of "The Place of the Jackals."

In 1932, the pottery pieces found by the eccentric hermit were shown to Van Graans, a Boer farmer and prospector. His curiosity fired, he induced an African to point out the place of the "sacred" precinct. Undeterred by the tangle of thornbush and scrub, the party made its way to the base of Mapungubwe. When they reached its precipitous flanks, the adventurers noticed that the previous hill dwellers had cut small holes in the wall facing, perhaps to accomodate a ladder.

Climbing laboriously, they finally emerged on the summit. Here they found a low facade of stone and some large, loose boulders which, they speculated, must have been used as protection against potential intruders. Faced with unwelcome visitors, the early dwellers could have pushed the boulders over the side to show their lack of hospitality.

The little party found beads, bits of iron and copper and pottery strewn about. Even more exciting was the fact that a recent cloudburst had exposed a piece of gold, which Van Graans quickly spotted as it lay glittering in the sun.

Later, Van Graans' son, a university student, reported the find to his professor, Leo Fouché. It was Fouché who described the ensuing events. In his report on the excavation made in 1937, the professor commented enthusiastically:

"This was a critical moment in the history of Mapungubwe."

He then went on to report how, on the first day of the archaeological examination spurred by Van Graans' adventure, a hasty and anxiety-filled search took place. The archaeologist found gold beads, bangles and small bits of gold plating. Poking about in the loose soil, they unearthed large sheets of gold plating, some bearing designs. One of the most striking discoveries was a tiny, gold-plate rhinoceros, thought to have been originally attached to a piece of wood. Also, a skeleton was unearthed, but even the most careful digging could not prevent its bones from crumbling as they came in contact with the air.

Fouché confirmed the value of the discovery by sending plate specimens to the Royal Mint, which declared unequivocally after examination that they were, indeed, of the purest gold. Fortunately for posterity, all of the gold discovered during these first and somewhat disorganized archaeological digs at Mapungubwe apparently has been accounted for and placed safely in museums.

Subsequently, others visited the site, which fast became a celebrated one. The South African government entrusted the University of Pretoria with the later investigation. Professor

Van Riet Lowe made an inspection and declared Mapungubwe a major and intact site. He noted one curious feature: an over-burden of some 10,000 tons of soil which looked as though it had been brought from elsewhere. Later, this phenomenon was explained by the fact that the mesa-top dwellers had a habit of heaping their village sites with earth. Every time a hut was burned, it was the custom of its owner in rebuilding to raise the floor level by a few feet. Apparently in the intervals between rebuilding, the level of the surrounding yard also was raised time and time again. In many cases, the floor level of the hut was lower than that of the surrounding yard. This process was revealed during examination and excavation by the thin, yellow lines of old floor surfaces which ran with bewildering intricacy along the side walls of the excavation trenches.

Grave areas were found subsequently by an excavator named Van Tonder. The graves, 23 in all, contained a large quantity of gold and other archaeologically important objects. Eventually, the Mapungubwe necropolis was scientifically authenticated as having been the royal burial ground long before the Europeans arrived in southern Africa. One skeleton had been buried with 70 ounces of gold. In addition to quantities of gold plating, the royal necropolis also yielded some 12,000 gold beads.

Despite the abundance and richness of these discoveries, it appears certain that a wealth of other artifacts, as well as historical information, still awaits further investigation on the table-top mountain site. This is borne out in part by Fouché's assertion that "up to June 1935, some 2,000 tons of midden had been examined; but on and around the hill there are probably 100,000 tons of midden which had not been touched." Furthermore, he observed that there was a disparity of evidence between the cultural material and the skeletal remains which the site had yielded up to that time. As one possible line of investigation, Fouché suggested that a team of perhaps a dozen archaeologists be assigned to establishing the date of the final fall of the Empire of Monomotapa. Such a clarification, he believed, might shed new light on Mapungubwe, which was thought to have been the southernmost province of the Shona's Monomotapa Empire.

One investigator, G.A. Gardner, continued working tenaciously at Mapungubwe until 1940. Yet after digesting the results of his field work, he conceded in 1955 that he was still unable to answer some of the most fascinating but vexing problems surrounding the site: who the people of the hill were, what their political organization had been and why they had taken up residence atop the isolated mesa.

Even now, the links between Mapungubwe and the Zimbabwe ruins are not clearly established. Pottery found scattered about the plains surrounding the former site are being investigated for further clues. Some of the recovered potshards have been reconstructed and found to be nearly identical in shape and apparent function with vessels still used by the indigenous population today. One type of receptical, for example, is styled for catching the dripping sap of the Malala palm, which is fermented to make a potent wine. This vessel is found most frequently today in the Limpopo Valley region, where the Malala palm luxuriates.

Some of the pottery suggests links with the ceramic ware of Leopolds Kopje, a distinct Iron Age group which inhabited Rhodesia at about the end of the first millennium. There were also other peoples, as yet unidentified by archaeologists, who inhabited the region around Mapungubwe. Whoever they were, it seems certain that their ancestors were the backbone of the Iron Age populations, for they controlled the mines of copper and gold. They have been described at least tentatively as having been tall, brown-skinned pastoralists. Whether they came to the region as conquerors or as refugees cannot be determined on the basis of present evidence.

The elaborate hill layout suggests that Mapungubwe was a place where important personalities had their day. Ironworking was practiced. Clay figurines were molded, although few human sculptures have been found. As we have seen, important burials were always accompanied by great numbers of gold-wire bangles. Bits of gold-plated head-rests have been excavated, as have a gold-plated bowl and the remains of a gold-tipped staff. What is remarkable is the fine craftsmanship that obviously went into the production of gold-plate. Most of the samples recovered were found to be of uniform thickness and free from holes which normally mar such workmanship when inexpertly done. Thus, the samples gave evidence of the great time and high skill expended--a level of craftsmanship scarcely rivaled by modern gold-beaters. Furthermore, it must be remembered that the Mapungubwe craftsmen worked with only the most primitive tools.

The economy of the Mapungubwe occupants was based on the cultivation of cereal crops, cattle and herds of small stock. There is little evidence that game was hunted for food, but vegetable produce seems to have been collected to supplement the diet. Flat-bladed arrowheads, spearheads and hoes were in evidence, but no ceremonial tools were found.

There are strong indications that an Iron Age population with a rich culture dominated by a Shona minority whose influence on their material existence became stronger as time went on. The oral tradition of the area's present-day Venda people, whose culture coincides with the Shona of Zimbabwe in many respects, speaks of the hill at Mapungubwe in religious ceremonies. To this day, the Venda are still terrified of the site. The Venda are a branch of the Sotho people, who occupy a considerable part of the interior of South Africa. Some think the Venda are remnants of the founders of Zimbabwe. The Sotho were part of the last wave of Bantu expansion which began around 1720 and continued until the entrance of the Europeans in 1801. In fact, the population of the Mapungubwe hill culture was probably purely Bantu.

The settlement shows no signs whatsoever of having been hastily abandoned or of being sacked. Although it is pure conjecture, Fouché made the observation that the site may have proved

undesirable and that its inhabitants simply left and dispersed in
an organized way. The burials atop the hill are dated rather late
in Mapungubwe history, probably shortly before the area was
abandoned following a very long occupancy. It is not impossible
that when the people decided to disperse, they buried their dead
chief with sacred objects which for them had, for some unknown
reason, lost their original significance.

Another of Fouché's speculations relates to the quality of
the occupants' daily lives. He thought that after so lengthy a period
in one place, the accumulation of decaying rubbish caused by the
inhabitants themselves made it unhealthy for them to remain there.
Present-day African tribes adjust to such a situation by simply
moving to an adjacent area. This may have been what happened
at Mapungubwe; their only alternative to being inundated in their
own litter may have been to move the entire settlement.

Other explorations in the area turned up signs of the Stone
Age. However, it appears that the Stone Age implements did not
originate on the site but were probably mixed in earth carried
there for a land-fill operation, possibly for the raising of hut floors
and yards. Rock paintings also were found in the vicinity, the beginning of what is called the polychrome development of cave art
practiced by the Late Stone Age Wilton Man of Rhodesia. These
paintings include buck, giraffe, locusts, human figures and a picture of an animal hide spread out to dry. Wilton Man no doubt
arrived on the scene earlier than the Bantu. He moved through
the area while giraffe roamed there, as indicated by the rock
paintings. And since it is a known fact that giraffe will not go
near human settlements, the evidence points to the conclusion
that in the Late Stone Age, the region was very thinly populated,
if at all.

ENGARUKA

The southward sweep of Bantu peoples which brushed Inyanga left other occupation traces--some more mysterious than

Zimbabwe. Engaruka is a case in point; only the uncomprehending breezes blow about its ruins. All that remains is the tantalizing remnants of village settlements, stone huts and a scattering of small houses that dot the eastern slopes of Mount Ngorongoro, very near the Kenya-Tanzania border. Who and what was there and why the occupants came, rose to eminence and vanished are puzzles which still elude archaeologists. It is not even known how old the ruins are.

There are, however, a few clues and much speculation. For example, the spread and stimulus of the Iron Age techniques mentioned earlier may be the framework within which to answer the question of Engaruka's rise to its peak. Also, the settlement was large, suggesting that it may have had a relationship with nearby peoples--a contact which may have been alternately cordial and hostile.

One theory of Engaruka's disappearance from history is that the people became the victims of intruders who moved into the land and destroyed the culture but were unable to replace it with anything approaching its previous level. Some authorities identify the invaders as the southward-moving Masai. In any case, the end came to the Iron Age settlement that was once complex, mature and, from all indications, achieved a high material level.

Lying as it does at the foot of the western wall of the Rift Valley, Engaruka is littered with stone enclosures, field systems, terraces, cairns, dams and furrows. The subject of a major excavation in 1964, it was found to be an advanced agricultural society.

Even the architecture and settlement planning show the overriding influence of agricultural requirements. Thus, houses were cut into one another as they rose tier on tier along the steep slopes. This construction would seem to be an example of response to environment; utilization of the precipitous slopes for housing freed a maximum of level land for cultivation--an essential consideration in a region of scanty rainfall. Overall, the ground plan suggests peasant farming circled about a main settlement.

Dr. Louis Leakey carried out a preliminary excavation in 1936 and estimated that the ruins were once a city of more than 30,000 inhabitants. His calculation was based on the finding that the site contained some 6,800 habitations. Leakey theorized that the site was chosen for its strategic position, which would seem to be advantageous for warding off any attackers.

Working on the theory of water consumption required for the approximately 800 acres available for cultivation, Leakey speculated that the desication of the region was the reason for abandonment. Under present conditions of rainfall, the population that he hypothesized at the time of maximum occupancy would have required 10 times the acreage that was actually available to support the inhabitants. This observation in part accounts for the current emphasis being placed on a shift in climate as the reason for Engaruka's abandonment. If it can be proved that the occupation coincided with a period of increasing aridity, it would seem reasonable to suppose that at some point the inhabitants moved away to settle where water was more readily available.

Engaruka shows evidence of having had at least a limited occupation for a long period of time during the second millenium A.D. It was thought to have been definitively abandoned in the 19th century owing to local disturbances.

There is reason to hope that further information about the ancient site may be gleaned from modern inhabitants of the region. For example, at a place called Sonjo, just northwest of Engaruka, the local Bantu peoples still employ irrigation methods to support groups of up to 800 people in a single village. In other ways, too, the Bantu live under circumstances very like those of the area's earlier inhabitants. Anthropological studies of today's population may eventually supplement archaeological evidence in helping to clarify the relationship between the modern peoples and those of Engaruka.

CHAPTER 7 CITIES ON THE SEA

". . . plenty of oranges, sweet and bitter."
Barbosa

"It is said," wrote Pliny, "that in the parts interior from the east coast there are people whose whole face is flat without a nose; who have no nostrils nor any opening in the face beyond a single hole through which they breathe..."

The historical features of Africa's east coast were scarcely better known up to 20 years ago than Pliny's credulous and fantastic conception of the peoples who lived away from the coast.

The door to the history of 2,500 years of coastal history was locked until the last century when a handful of pioneering scholars provided a key through their research. They include J. Kirkman, Dr. G.S.P. Freeman-Grenville, Dr. Roland Oliver and Dr. A.G. Mathew. Yet even with the output of this dedicated few, it must be admitted that the history of the east coast of Africa up to the 13th and 14th centuries is virtually unknown. As Kirkman put it, even now it is "largely a matter of inspired interpretation."

The oldest surviving document relating to coastal history is the "Periplus of the Erythrean Sea," a log compiled in A.D. 110. The Erythrean Sea was the Indian Ocean; sometimes the east coast region was referred to as "the territory of Erythrean Africa." The author of this log was a Greek from Alexandria who lived during the Emperor Nero's reign. He was an officer on a merchant ship and traveled the Indian Ocean as a commercial representative of a company which operated from Berenice on the Red Sea.

The "Periplus" was a route book and handy guide of factual information intended for traders. Although archaeologists are still trying to identify and locate all of the places mentioned in the 7,500-word text of "Periplus," some are clearly decipherable.

77

Thus, it was in this document that the name "Azania" was given currency as the Greek designation for Africa's east coast. Today, the word has echoes in the name of a modern African state, the United Republic of Tanzania. And a city called Rhapta, whose location long puzzled "Periplus" scholars, is believed to have been found at the Pangani estuary on the Tanzanian coast north of Dar-es-Salaam. Rhapta was known to have belonged to the Roman sphere of influence at the time of Ptolemy in the second century B.C. and was then thought to be the end of the world.

The "Periplus" emerges as a series of regular maritime runs, listing the ports of call, markets and the products to be obtained in each. The political climate, information useful to traders then as now, is mentioned in passing. The guidebook says that the "far side ports" marked the customary route from Egypt-- presumably meaning that it was usual to sail to the East African market towns by way of the Red Sea and the Gulf of Aden, perhaps putting in at southern Arabian ports. In this way, the seagoing merchants could trade with Indian ships and thus work their way profitably down the African coast.

In their chronicles of the 11th and 12th dynasties, the ancient Egyptians call the coastal region south of the Horn of Africa "the Land of Punt." The Sabaeans are the most likely contenders for the honor of having been the first to sail around the Horn, making the long passage to the Azanian coast. To them, Azania meant roughly the coasts of Somalia, Kenya, and Tanganyika, including the ports of Kisimayu and Kilwa and the twin islands of Zanzibar and Pemba.

The Greeks speak in their chronicles of the wealth of the Sabaean traders--a wealth based on profits from the Indian and East African trade. Greek geographers of the second century B.C. mention the Sabaean Lane, then a well-traveled trade route. Greek ships first pressed around Cape Guardafui, the tip of the African Horn, in the reign of Ptolemy III (247-221 B.C.). They were searching for ivory and spices. This commercial demand explains the presence of ports in the Horn of Africa area.

EASTERN AFRICA

Adulis
Axum
Lake Tana
Cape Guardafui

White Nile R.
Blue Nile R.

Juba R.

Lake Rudolph

Mogadishu
Brava

Lake Victoria
Olduvai
Engaruka
Gedi
Lamu
Malindi
Mombasa
Pemba Island
Zanzibar

Congo R.

Pangani R.

S
W
A
H
I
L
I

C
O
A
S
T

INDIAN
OCEAN

Lake Tanganyika

Mafia Island
Kilwa

Cape Delgardo

Lake Nyasa

MADAGASCAR

Zambezi R.
Monomotapa
Empire
Inyanga
Zimbabwe
Khami
Sofala
Mapungubwe

0   250   500
SCALE OF MILES

Limpopo R.

Kalahari Desert

Map by Dino Lowenstein

The Graeco-Roman exploitation of the coast was the result of Hippalus' discovery and explanation in A.D. 47 of the intricacies of the monsoon winds. The plotting of the northeast monsoon conditioned the economic development of the East African ports, for it created conditions for commercial activity through which prosperity and cultural diffusion took place. The main sailing period seems to have been the season of the northeast monsoon in the northern Indian Ocean. Travel during this period was safer and more flexible because the skies were clear, for the most part, and there were light winds and active land and sea breezes.

The air mass of which this crucial wind is made up originates in the dynamic anticyclone located over South Asia and the northern waters of the Indian Ocean. In the summer months, heat coming low over the land masses of South Asia controls air circulation in the lower atmosphere. By September, sufficient cooling allows tropical continental air to subside from above and begin to replace the tropical maritime air of the Indian Ocean. An intertropical front comes between these two air masses which, at its most northerly position in July, runs between the Sudan and Ethiopia, across South Arabia, Baluchistan, the Punjab and the Ganges Basin, into Upper Burma and, finally, Yunnan. Then it begins to retreat southward accompanied by dust storms which occur over northeast Africa. Frontal disturbances and rain squalls are experienced over the ocean at the same time. Dry continental air with a northeast component flows in its wake across the northern waters of the Indian Ocean.

In October, the intertropical front extends across the Arabian Sea and the Bay of Bengal. In the east, it may reach as far south as the equator. The Bay of Bengal then experiences treacherous weather with calm, clear periods giving way to violent hurricanes. But in the Arabian Sea, there are extended periods of fine, settled weather; and in the Gulf of Aden and the southern parts of the Red Sea, easterly winds are established in the middle of October.

It was because of these easterlies that so many outside elements populated the African shores, sometimes with rich and many-sided cultural traditions. Whenever past historians thought of Africa, it had always been in terms of the Persian and Arab coastal settlers, who had become prominent there. Credit was never given to the Africans for the original settlements. But as study progresses, other evidence has emerged to show that Africans did, indeed, play key roles in their own history in no way inferior to that of outsiders.

The earliest populations of the coast consisted of peoples of the Bushman type, whose culture, labeled Stillbay, was characterized by leaf-shaped, pointed implements which archaeologists have found scattered about the coast. These early peoples inhabited the dry savanna country, practiced a mixed economy, lived in small groups and did not travel far from the settlements.

They were followed by the Bantu, who arrived as early as the middle of the first millennium A.D. How they came remains a matter of debate; but it is thought that they reached the coast from the south, coming down the rivers of Portuguese East Africa and then moving north along the coastal plain.

Their earliest settlements are thought to have been purely Bantu societies which, at the time of foreign immigration, were gradually being turned toward Islam through the presence of many Persian and Arab traders. This was happening long before the Persians and Arabs decided to make the coastal strip their home.

Not unnaturally, the documents written in Arabic tend to record this "conquest" in the historical light most favorable to the newcomers. Arab reports do not reflect the state of mind of the Africans during that time.

The prosperity of the coast depended on the gold of the interior that was mined around Zimbabwe. Yet so terrified were the early traders by such imaginative if inaccurate accounts as

Pliny's that they never dared to enter the interior. Instead, they worked out a system of intermediaries to bring to the coast the coveted commodities that the interior produced: copper, gum ivory, leopard skins, tortoise shell, rhinoceros horn and slaves.

Among the earlier inhabitants of the region were the Galla, who--together with the Somali, the Bantu and Arabs--are the component parts of the present-day coastal population. The Galla are a Hamitic people whose language is related to that of the Arabs. They are said to have come across the Red Sea from South Arabia as early as 1000 B.C. but later were pushed south and west by movements of the Somali. The Galla, a pastoral people, displaced the Bushman hunters, the very earliest inhabitants. Whenever the Galla came in contact with the Bantu, they made them dependent on them, even though there was considerable intermarriage between the two groups.

In a very interesting way, the Galla accomplished a borrowing from their early forebears. It is in the construction of their houses which reflects that of the East African hunters who preceded them in the area. The Galla house is hemispherically shaped and can be easily taken along, together with other accoutrement, in their pastoral wanderings. The house is made of bent poles set in the ground in a circle. The poles are fastened together at the top and then covered with brush or hides.

Among themselves, the Galla enjoy an egalitarian relationship in the modern sense of the word; there is no hereditary aristocracy. The Galla people overran southern Ethiopia and most of the Kenya coast, coming to within a few miles of Mombasa. In the 19th century, they were attacked by the Masai and Somali, after which they withdrew northward.

Following in the path of the Galla people came the Somali, a branch of the Hamite stock, who settled along the south shores of the Gulf of Aden. Responding to the foreign influences of the early 10th century, they showed great enthusiasm for Islam and intermarried quite harmoniously with the Arabs. In the early part of the second millennium A.D., they successfully drove the Galla southward and dominated the agricultural Bantu, who were once dependent on the Galla of the Webbe Shebeli, in Somaliland. The Somali first seized the Bantu land and then subjugated the farmers.

From A.D. 575 to 879, the Persians were involved in wresting the valuable coastal trade away from the Arabs. It was the Persians who had stretched the trading arm eastward to include China.

Since antiquity, the Chinese had been well advanced in their knowledge of sailing and navigational techniques and were therefore particularly amenable to trade. There is no doubt of their early voyages to the east coast of Africa. There are numerous--though sometimes vague--references in the literature of China to substantiate these maritime exploits. A text of the early Han dynasty (202 to 9 B.C.) refers to various voyages, but the accounts are not geographically precise enough to trace definitively. The earliest document specifically mentioning East Africa is dated 1060. It is an extract from an earlier work, dated 863-- a time when Arab traders already were active and well-established in Canton. The most detailed and therefore the most useful of all such documents was written by a trade commissioner of China at Ch'uan-chou in Fukien; the text was completed in 1226. Another record is that of the Admiral Ch'ang-lo, whose ships plied the Somali coastline from 1418 to 1432, the time of the Ming dynasty. One Chinese traveler to the coast reported that "from olden times on, they were not subject to any country." Another, Chang Hseih, cautioned travelers to master the sea and take care against those "greedy of gain."

There is clear archaeological evidence of early Chinese participation in the African east coast trade. Chinese coins from the eighth century have been unearthed at Kilwa on the Kenya coast and at Mogadishu in Somalia.

Sir Mortimer Wheeler, the British archaeologist, says that the luxury goods which became common on the coast were bought not with the profits of trade carried on along the East Coast but from the proceeds of the interior Southern Rhodesian gold trade, from which Kilwa served as an entrepot.

The late fourth to the late seventh centuries were most crucial to the history of the coast, and it is for this period that the information is fragmentary. In the early fourth and fifth centuries, direct contact between the Mediterranean and Indian Ocean gradually diminished. This was due either to Persian economic dominance or to the commercial ascendancy of Axum. At this time, the western half of the Indian Ocean was controlled by the Sassanian dynasty of the Persian Empire. The Sassanian kings, rulers of Mesopotamia and the Persian area around the fourth century, had built up a considerable sea power. It is thought that they were stimulated by the rivalry between the pearl fisheries at Bahrain, which lay within their Persian Gulf sphere of influence, and those of southern India. It is clear that at the death of King Shapur II in 379, Persia was a dominant sea power. In the reign of Bahram V (420-439), Persia actually controlled the seas in the western half of the Indian Ocean. She maintained this hold until the Sassanian Empire was destroyed by the Moslems in 643.

The early Arab accounts of their East African coastal settlements say that it was in the opening centuries of Islam--coinciding with the seventh and eighth centuries of the Christian era--that the existing ports of Mogadishu and Kilwa were incorporated into the Islamic world. However, this date is thought to be far too early and the 13th century is probably a closer approximation.

The 13th century was a time of great trial in the eastern and western parts of the Islamic world. Religious disagreements abounded. These were bitter days for some. Questions of faith ran high and many exiles and fugitives were created by sharp political as well as religious disagreements. Many left home with the idea that it would be less difficult to earn a living elsewhere.

So the dissidents and discontented emigrated to the coast of Africa. They were people plucked from the very heart of civilized centers: artisans, craftsmen and scholars. These newcomers settled in Africa, raised multiracial families and founded the first colonial towns on the coast: at Mogadishu, Barawa, Lamu, Pate, Malindi, Mombasa, Kilwa, Sofala and old Zanzibar.

A new conglomerate of peoples arose as the result of the marriages of Arab and Persian settlers. They came to be known as the "Sawahila," or "coastalists." Another result of this convergence of human forces was a common language along the Banadir (Somali) coast. The lingua franca was necessitated by the need to communicate from settlement to settlement. Where there were regional variations, what emerged was Swahili, a language incorporating the speech of the Bantu of northern Somali and having strong elements of Arabic.

Through these various interactions, a Bantu-Islamic civilization evolved. It was molded by the Arab and Persian immigrants, but it preserved the distinctly Bantu features of these early settlers.

The port settlements were not so much "cities" or "states" at this time but rather a nuclei of nonterritorially defined power systems. The history of the East African littoral is one of powerful and ambitious families who organized towns. These communities decayed at times but were later refounded. Some grew into city-states, but they never were a political whole. The texture of coastal life was greatly enhanced by the non-African aliens who reorganized the life and added new conceptions of art. For example, they revolutionized the architecture of tropical Africa.

Some of the migrations were organized. The most notable of these was that of the Almozaid, the Shirazi of Kilwa, the Suleiman brothers of Lamu and the Nabahani of Pate. The Almozaid apparently failed to organize an on-going political structure, but the Shirazi and Nabahini were the founders of the most integrated states on the coast. Islam was the spirit which permeated the whole.

Kilwa was one such state to become an urban polity. It was originally built in the 10th century A.D. by immigrants who had been driven out of Oman at the end of the seventh century A.D. The earliest attempt at colonization, according to the Pate Chronicle, was from Persia and not Arabia. This story is quasi-historical. According to the Chronicle, Abdulmalik, the fifth of the Umayyad caliphs (A.D. 695-703), had heard of East Africa and "his soul longed to found a new kingdom." After considering the idea, he sent "Syrians" to build cities along the African coast. One such city was said to have been on Zanzibar Island. The Chronicle goes on to say that after Abdulmalik died, his sons had no interest in carrying on the work of founding towns and so they abandoned them to languish unfinished.

The Arabic version of the Kilwa Chronicle (one of two from antiquity, the other being in Portuguese) speaks of a large immigration from Shiraz in Persia to East Africa. The story relates that a sultan of Shiraz called Hassan bin Ali dreamed that he saw a rat with an iron snout nibbling at his house. He felt that the walls of his house were surely threatened. The sultan interpreted the dream as foretelling the downfall of his kingdom. Because of these gloomy predictions, which he thoroughly believed, Hassan bin Ali joined his six sons in seven dhows and sailed to East Africa. The father and sons eventually settled in different spots along the coast, including Kilwa and offshore Pemba. This was in A.D. 985.

In about A.D. 1035, the Chronicle continues, Hassan bin Suleiman became the Sultan of Kilwa. After having ruled for about 12 years, he was driven from his royal palace by an African tribe, which put in his place another Arab as governor. Kilwa remained under this occupation regime for 12 years. All during this time, the people were planning to restore Hassan bin Suleiman, who had obviously escaped to Zanzibar. But upon his return to Kilwa, the sultan was slain. Eventually, however, his allies managed to seize the usurper and place the sultan's son in charge.

The story of the migration of the Shiraz sultan and his six sons probably refers to an account of a Shirazi movement from the Somali coast southward, where they displaced the local inhabitants. The northern settlements began to decline as a result of population shifts to the south owing to a change in trade patterns. Emigration further south along the coast was attributable to the fact that these areas were thriving.

It wasn't until the 14th century that a Shirazi coastal civilization as such could claim to have been definitely established. Before this time, there was still movement between the home country and the coastal lands. Many of the early settlements are situated on the isles off the coast for very good reason. These islands protected the settlers against the incursions from mainland tribes.

Besides the unsettling factor of not being completely welcome, the Persian newcomers were subject to the imponderables of the trading economy. They neither had control of the economic climate on which they so much depended nor did they take to the humid and enervating weather of the coast. These settlements and people flourished or dimmed in response to local changes. They were attacked frequently, and they sustained these attacks according to their varying abilities to protect themselves.

Another problem was that they had no organization within the region in which they were so precariously settled. The ruins in themselves are mute testimony to the transitory nature of these settlements. In time, the towns declined, and there is no indication of either their names or length of life. Gedi is one place whose site at least is marked, although little else is known about it.

The growth of Kilwa is not legend but is confirmed by the finding of coins which are both a record and a survey of the last 2,000 years of coastal history. In the 13th century, Ali bin al-Hasan started to mint his own coins. It is known that coins had also been struck by the 13th century at Zanzibar and at Mogadishu, on the Somali coast. These kings struck their coins in copper. There names were inscribed, but no dates were included. A cache of silver coins, which he believed were linked with the 13th century in Kilwa, was found by archaeologist Neville Chittick in 1964.

The length and breadth of coastal trade can be delineated from these and other coin finds, which include Hellenistic samples from the third to first centuries B.C. to Roman, Byzantine and Mongol pieces and Chinese coins minted under the T'ang, Sung, Ming and Ching dynasties. Others originated in Ceylon and southern India.

Reconciling archaeological finds with history is the major academic problem of piecing together coastal history. Excavations reveal that Kilwa and Mafia, an offshore island port, were substantial settlements long before Ali bin al-Hasan arrived.

It is thought that the area was occupied for three centuries and that during the latter part of this period there was a considerable number of Moslems at Kilwa and Mafia. All the towns were pagan before A.D. 1100. There may have been mosques and worshipers in that neighborhood; but possible because of perishable building materials, that part of the story has been obliterated. These early non-Moslems traded with the East, but purely in the role of an entrepot; they themselves produced nothing for export.

Gervase Mathew, a British archaeologist, made some important discoveries on a group of small islands off southern Tanzania. On the isle of Janje ya Kati, near Kilwa, he found hidden in dense underbrush the ruins of a settlement which he described as consisting of "small, oblong houses of carefully dressed masonry, grouped around a citadel whose walls still rise to 16 feet." This is the earliest of the coastal settlements found so far. It is thought to be pre-Islamic and to have been iron-using. Not far away on Song Marna, an island of coral, Mathew was suddenly given the opportunity to speculate on the scope of early trade. For here he examined and identified glazed stoneware, almost certainly from Thailand (Siam), and a mass of Chinese porcelain dating from the late Sung to early Ming dynasties (A.D. 1127-1450). Mathew also found coins from Mesopotamic and Mongol mints in Persia, pierced carnelians from India, amber, crystal and topaz -- all of it screened by the coral island's mangrove swamps. The commerce of the whole world of the East added to the flavor of Song Marna's streets and filled its warehouses.

The earliest antiquities found thus far are at the lowest excavation level at Kilwa. They consisted of debris left behind by a people who ate fish and who either camped or lived in temporary huts on a sandspit. Fishermen that move about frequently on the coast today do not live too dissimilarly.

Although it does not mean they did not exist, no permanent houses were found at the lowest level of excavation. Indeed, not long after the original excavations, it was discovered that mud houses were built on sand. Fashioned with a red subsoil obtained from the eastern part of Kilwa Island, they were plastered on a framework of vertical poles and horizontal rods. These materials and this style of building continued to dominate construction for several centuries.

No one knows how large the settlement was, but it appears to have covered a large area. Tin-glazed Islamic pottery, probably imported from Mesopotamia, turned up in one of the layers. This find was ascribed to the ninth or possibly the 10th century. This suggests that the earliest Kilwa camps could date back as far as the eighth century. There are no radiocarbon dates to confirm or refute this hypothesis. Other Islamic pottery of differing styles has been found along with a few pieces of Chinese porcelain. Sir Mortimer Wheeler expresses the opinion that the entire history of the east coast can be read in the porcelain finds. Flasks of glass and vessels of soapstone, all of mysterious origin, also were found.

The new stratum yielded the information that stone buildings were fairly commonplace. The construction material was coral stone. Later, floors made of lime plaster show up; and not long thereafter, lime plaster was used on the walls. At other places, not far away, mosques were found with flat roofs supported by pillars. This period, with its coursed-stone building development, coincided with the Shirazi migration from the Banadir coast to Mafia and Kilwa.

A fresh influx of immigrants in the second half of the 13th century took place along with an upsurge in the wealth and prosperity of Kilwa. The gold trade with the port of Sofala was expanding, and the sultans were prime beneficiaries.

Ibn Battuta in 1331 recalls:

"The Island is quite separate from the mainland. It grows bananas, lemons and oranges...The people do not engage in agriculture but import grain from the Swahili."

He added that their mosques were made of wood and that the worshipers followed the Shafi'i rite and "are devout, chaste and virtuous." The inhabitants are black, he observed.

"Kilwa," he said in summary, "is one of the most beautiful and well-constructed towns in the world. The whole of it is elegantly built."

It was during this time that the previously built Great Mosque at Kilwa was greatly extended. It is wholly different in its architecture from its predecessors.

A huge structure was uncovered near Kilwa in 1947, further evidence of the city's prosperity. It is thought that the structure was a ruler's residence and is perhaps the largest pre-European building in Africa after Zimbabwe. It is known as Husani Kubwa ("big Husani"). Nearby, there is another structure, called Husani Ndogo ("little Husani"). The Husanis are in an isolated position and are distinctive in character. It was thought at first that part of this huge area of two acres was used for commercial purposes--that is, a kind of "factory." However, this speculation has not yet been established.

Coins made their appearance during this period, which coincided with the Shirazi migration from the Banadir coast to Kilwa and Mafia. They were struck locally in the mint of Ali bin al-Hasan. This earliest type of coin had a nan.e and, oddly enough, a rhyming phrase on the obverse side, each written in one line. Subsequent types of coins from the same mint had the name written on two lines. The name is inscribed in angular script ending with flourishes and appears similar to floriated Kufic script. A pot containing 570 coins of this type was found leaning against the wall of a mosque in 1964. This cache was unearthed at Mafia and is the most striking evidence that these coins were of the earliest type. The pot of coins which has helped us to spin the historical yarn of the coast was found in sand which had accumulated against the wall of the mosque. They were in good condition. Apart from this hoard, even more coins dated from the middle or end of the 13th century were found at Mafia and Kilwa.

Kilwa declined in the mid-14th century. There seems to have been a small recovery in the 15th century when some large buildings decorated with Islamic and porcelain bowls set in their roofs were constructed. No coins were minted by the sultans of this period.

By the time the Portuguese arrived there, Kilwa's high point had been reached, and she had fallen into decline. Barbosa, arriving home in Portugal in 1518, thought that he had seen Kilwa at its best. It is supposed that Barbosa sailed in 1500 with Pedro Alvares Cabral, who had reached East Africa on a voyage from Portugal after a detour in which he discovered Brazil.

There is a narrative relating to the voyage, published in 1938 by the Hakluyt Society. It is called "The Voyages of Pedro Alvares Cabral." Cabral describes the African coastal peoples as black men and adds that "in this land, there are rich merchants, and there is much gold and silver and amber and musk and pearls." The inhabitants, he observes, dressed in garments "of fine cotton and silk." This Portuguese mariner literally wrecked the trade of Kilwa, and the port was never able to re-capture the commercial prosperity of former times. As Kilwa's fortunes languished, Mombasa's position rose.

Mombasa is an oval-shaped island--a coral atoll that rises in places to an altitude of 50 feet. The word "Mombasa" is said to derive from the Arab root "nabas," meaning roughly "to speak in public" and, by extension, a place of congress for other than trading purposes. The legendary King of Zenj was thought to have lived there, and the traveling Arab geographer Ibn Battuta spent the night in Mombasa in 1332.

One theory worth pondering in relation to Kilwa until ex-cavations invalidate or confirm it is that of J. S. Trimingham. He suggests that the Shirazi civilization did not come directly from Persia or the Persian Gulf. He thinks that these migrants grew up on East Africa's Banadir coast and that when they finally moved southward toward Mafia and Kilwa, the migration was, in fact, a movement of Swahilized people from Banadir. They may have settled on the coast, calling themselves Shirazi in much the same way that the Swahili people of Zanzibar do to this day. So, too, the Persian tradition has its tantalizing evidence. Flags that once were flown by the now-extinct "sewn" boats (mtepe) are con-nected with that of a "Persian" sultan, Al-Shungwaya, who is thought to be identical with the founder of the Kilwa dynasty. The Shirazi dynasty began at Kilwa in A.D. 1200.

Vasco da Gama landed at Gedi on April 13, 1498. It was located just 65 miles north of Mombasa and 10 miles south of Ma-lindi. Gedi was founded in the 13th century and prospered from the 14th to the 16th centuries. Gedi, or Gede, is a term meaning "precious." The port was one of the largest surviving Arab co-lonial towns and the only one maintained as a public resort. Game proliferated there. Elephants, rhinoceros, ostrich and giraffe were commonplace.

The only tomb found at the site is dated at A.D. 1399, cor-responding to the Hegira year 802. Gedi's earliest pottery shards are of a glazed earthenware with the pattern scratched through the glaze. This is known as sgraffiato.

Gedi is thought to have been destroyed in the 16th century, when climatic conditions seem to have shifted in the area. The evidence of climatic change may also suggest a reason for the dwindling of the east coast African civilizations in the late 16th and 17th centuries. It has been shown that after a period of exceptionally good rainfall, a drying up took place.

Although it did not appear from John Kirkman's excavation at Gedi that violence had occurred, it was clear that Gedi's builders made a sudden departure. The Galla, who apparently were in retreat after having been attacked by another African tribe called the Giriama, might have forced out the occupants of Gedi. The Galla were a nomadic cattle-keeping people who had a natural dislike of towns. Their policy was one of extermination, and they were in the area at the time. They would not have bothered to either assimilate or exploit those whom they had subdued or conquered. There is no doubt that the Arabs and the Bantu of Gedi retreated before the spears of the Galla.

Gedi is now abandoned and its ruins are overgrown with a small forest. Honey gatherers and archaeologists are the only ones to penetrate the ancient precincts. Over the years, the site has acquired a reputation for housing spirits and ghosts. Dr. Kirkman confesses that although "archaeologists are not spiritualists, since their feet are so firmly on the ground," he noted a "peculiar aura" surrounding the place, which he said caused him to keep looking over his shoulder. This aura, he adds, was neither friendly nor hostile.

CHAPTER 8 ISLAND OUTPOSTS

"The people...come to the country of the Zenjs
in large and small ships."

Edrisi

Although geographically separate from Africa, two of the
continent's insular appendages belong to any consideration of the
east coast's historical and cultural development.

One is Zanzibar, an island of 640 square miles lying 23
miles off the coast. It is traditionally considered together with
its satellite, the 380-square-mile island of Pemba, 25 miles to
the northeast.

The second offshore cultural center is Madagascar. Meas-
uring roughly 980 miles long and 360 miles wide, it is separated
from the continent by the broad Mozambique Channel.

Zanzibar takes its name from the term "Zanj," which the
early travelers from Arabia used to designate the coastal peoples
of East Africa. Masudi says that the word "Zanj" is of mysterious
origin. It is thought that the term was first mentioned in a Persian
inscription dating from 293 B.C. which records that King Narseh
had contacts with "Zhand Afrik Shah." It is still not known to
whom the Persian king was referring.

At some yet undetermined date, the Bantu came to Zanzibar. Their arrival is thought to have occurred at a very remote
time and that even then there might well have been indigenous inhabitants to greet them. The earliest peoples who lived on Zanzibar could have been a long-headed Negroid type with a protrud-
ing jaw and a small brain case--actually an ancestoral form of
man. Fossil finds in South Africa strongly suggest that there may
be a connection between the primordial populations of South Africa
and Zanzibar.

93

At Pemba, there is a traditional story which recalls that the island was once inhabited by a race of men said to have been gigantic in stature. These tallest of men were called the "Mengenge." At one point, the Bantu overran them. The giants have been credited with building the mosques that were later found on Pemba. There is no evidence to support what would seem to be an exaggeration characteristic of the times, although admittedly archaeological work on the island is still in its infancy.

In the "Periplus," the writer asserts that "along the coast live men of piratical habits, very great in stature and under separate chiefs in each place." It is likely that the story reflects the common practice of an invading people magnifying the attributes-- often the physical stature--of their adversaries to inflate their own conquests. Certainly, while related by a common language, the Bantu differ among themselves physically--but not to the extent of producing a race of giants.

Early artifacts that have come to light on Zanzibar so far have been scanty, although of immense historical value. These include coins, now housed in the Beit al-Amani Museum, from the time of the Roman Emperors Diocletian and Licinius and Emperor Justinian of Byzantium. Also unearthed have been five Parthian pieces from the mint of Ctesiphon, of which the latest is attributed to the reign of Ardashir (A.D. 212-241). Two Hellenistic coins from the second century A.D. are also in the collection. The museum also displays glass beads of Roman manufacture dating from about the same period.

There is proof of a non-African presence near Kisimkazi, situated at the southern end of Zanzibar. It is the mosque of Dimbani Kisimkazi, architectural evidence supported by local legend that a settlement once existed at the site. Certainly, the religious connotation and the artistic style of the mosque leave no doubt of an outside source of inspiration. The ruins indicate that the mosque was an architectural gem. And local oral tradition has it that the house of worship was not the work of Africans, although by this time many of the prosperous families of the coast had intermarried with the coastal Swahili.

The story of the mosque's construction has been handed down by word of mouth from one generation to the next--at times a remarkably accurate means of transmitting history. The story is that the Sultan of Kiza, founder of the settlement, employed a slave named Kizi to be his architect and aide. From the moment the work began, it took on such a glorious outline that it excited the envy of a neighboring chieftain, who sent an emissary to demand that Kiza hand over this valuable slave to him. Kiza flatly refused.

Infuriated, the jealous chieftain then resolved to take the slave by force. He sent his troops by dhow and closed in by sea on Kiza's domain. Though immersed in the mosque-building operation, Kiza recognized his danger as the enemy flotilla moved into sight. In great distress, he prayed for divine assistance, and his prayers were answered. Miraculously, a great swarm of bees suddenly materialized and drove off the enemy.

Undeterred by this misfortune, the rival chieftain tried again. This time he decided on an overland approach. The operation was so successful that the sultan had no advance warning of the new invasion threat and was unable to ask for a second divine intervention. Instead, he had a premonition. He suddenly felt-- "out of a clear blue sky," it is said--that defeat was upon him. Surrendering to fate, he made one last gesture of defiance: he cut off the right hand of his architect.

Then, hurrying to the shore which was the site of the mosque, the sultan prayed that he might be removed from this earth. In response, the ground opened beneath Kiza and engulfed him. It then closed, thrusting up a rock to mark his grave. To this day, the local inhabitants point out the rock and the scars of the crevice as the tomb of the Sultan of Kiza.

Whatever the truth of the matter, the fact is that Sheikh es-Said Imran Musa, the Kiza of the legend, has a prayer engraved on the wall of the mosque suggesting that he did not live in harmony with his neighbors.

MADAGASCAR

South of Zanzibar in the Indian Ocean lies Madagascar. The fourth largest island in the world, it has a population of about 4 million. Although to a large extent homogeneous in language and culture, the inhabitants are ethnically a highly complex mixture including varying degrees of Negroid, Mongoloid and Caucasoid peoples.

Theories abound (and conflict) as to the origins of the various races. The white racial element is in the minority and is mainly noticeable among the peoples of the coastal regions where history confirms European or Arab settlement. The main body of Madagascar's population, called the Malagasy, are a mixture of Malay (Mongoloid) with a strong infusion of Arab (Caucasoid) and a weak element of Bantu (Negroid). So far the island has not revealed skeletal remains of any other racial type nor is there indication of another culture in any way different from that of present-day Madagascar, now the Malagasy Republic.

On the other hand, clues that link Madagascar to the lands of the eastern Indian Ocean are plentiful. One of the most convincint cases concerns the local boat design. The mtepe used in Madagascar is clearly built along the Malay lines unquestionably borrowed from Indonesia. This vessel is constructed of planks lashed together with coconut-fiber cordage. It is propelled by rectangular mat sails. Decorating the bow and stern are round oculi, the "guiding eyes" commonly painted on primitive vessels. Another example of a local boat design harking back to an Indonesian source is the dau, a dugout canoe with double outriggers connected with the boom by indirect attachments. It is common along the East African coast, in Zanzibar and Madagascar and in the Bajun and Comoro Islands.

It is assumed that the Malays, or perhaps the Maanyan people from south-central Borneo, reached the East African coast shortly before the Christian era. They did not sail directly across the Indian Ocean but followed a coastwise course by way of India and southern Arabia, finally picking up the African coast in the Gulf of Aden, possibly somewhere around Cape Guardafui, the easternmost tip of the Horn of Africa. These early maritime adventurers left no records, either oral or written, to indicate why they left the Indonesian archipelago. It may have taken nothing more than the spirit of exploration, coupled with the search for trade opportunities, to launch them on their odyssey; for they had early developed skills in navigating outrigger canoes and used this skill to travel and trade with their southeast Asian neighbors.

"The Periplus of the Erythraean Sea" makes several references that lead us to assume that more than a whiff of Indonesian influence wafted to East Africa's coast. The chronicle mentions, for example, the coconut--a Malayan plant--as well as trade in coconut oil. It also mentions "sewed boats" and "canoes hollowed from a single log." These strongly suggest water craft originating in Indonesia.

There is abundant other evidence of the Malay people's presence on Africa's east coast. To name only three clues, there are a zither, an eel pot and a method of catching sea turtles--all imports to Africa from the southeast Asian archipelago.

In the 12th century, Edrisi, an Arab geographer, furnished further testimony to the presence of colonies of Malayo-Polynesian-speaking peoples along the east coast of Africa.

"The people of the isles of Zabag (Indonesia)," Edrisi wrote, "come to the country of the Zenjs (East Africa's coastal peoples) in large and small ships. They trade with them and export the Zenj merchandise, for they understand each other's language."

Similar historical accounts of Indonesians in East Africa abound until the 12th century, after which they cease.

In the plateau area of Madagascar, the traditions and gene-alogies of the Merina tribe ascribe the beginning of their ruling caste, the Andriana, to a second-millennium migration. These people were of a fairer skin than the Malay coastal peoples. There does not seem to be a special or separate migration from Indo-nesia to account for this phenomenon.

The peoples of Madagascar are divided into 11 major tribal groupings. They live in four areas differentiated in their basic economies. Geographically, the areas are the interior plateau, the east coast, the escarpment between them and the plains of the west coast, which includes the extreme north and south of the island.

In general, the social organization of the Malagasy, like their economy, clearly reflects their Indonesian ancestors. The early Indonesian coastal settlers brought with them rice, which was not accepted by the local people who were not familiar with the slash-and-burn method of agriculture necessary for rice cul-tivation at the time. However, for the immigrant settlers them-selves, rice was a staple crop almost from the beginning.

The Malagasy kingship system contrasts with that of the Arabs and the Bantu. And to add to the complexity of the Mala-gasy culture, the people have a tradition of a queen-mother and a queen-consort. This seems to be a pattern rather widespread in Africa and harks back to the time of Pharaonic Egypt. It is also speculated that this tradition may derive from more immedi-ate African sources, such as the traditions of the Ugandans and southwestern Ethiopians.

The banana, taro and yam, introduced by the Malagasy, were to affect the economic and cultural development of Africa as a whole over the centuries. They had become the staple food of the West African coastal tribes when the first Europeans set foot there. These plants point up in a pedestrian but definitive way the unity of African history continent-wide. There are wild yams in West Africa, although they are not of the Malay types. The banana did not originate in Africa, because those species present are cultivated and are complex hybrids of the wild forms, which are from India and Malaya. No wild form of the taro is known to grow in Africa. This plant cannot have been carried to the West Coast by sea--that is, around the Cape of Good Hope-- because the coastal East Africans, the Malagasy and later the Arabs never sailed further south than Mozambique. Nor is there any evidence that any early mariners sailing in the opposite direction anticipated the Portuguese navigators who first rounded the Cape. The conclusion would seem to be that these crops, which link the two coasts of Africa via the interior, must have diffused by land from east to west.

CHAPTER 9 PORTUGUESE INTERLUDE

"It is better to be a jackal at large than a greyhound
bound with a golden leash."

Sultan of Kilwa

The ivory, apes and peacocks brought back for King Solomon so that he "exceeded all the kings of the earth for riches"
were, in fact, the results of the southern African commerce made
famous from the good king's own records.

The coast was used as a refuge by Moslems from Oman,
who were forced to flee as the result of heated religious disagreements. Others with similar problems also came from Arabia.
The stimulus of these schisms and their effects must have provided the scholars of the day with a great spur to travel and see
what had formerly been beyond the bounds of their direct knowledge.

One such person was Masudi, a geographer who was born
in Baghdad toward the end of the ninth century. He sailed in A.D.
912 from Oman for Africa's east coast. As a result, he is regarded as one of the most informed eyewitnesses of the medieval
world. For some 40 years after his voyage, he penned his travel
observations. Ibn Khaldun, the great historian of the Arab world,
wrote some four centuries later that Masudi was "the model of
all historians." Masudi's famous work, called "The Meadows of
Gold and the Mines of Gems," was intended to excite the curiosity of his readers. The author wanted others to be fired with his
own burning interest in history. It is in this work that he described his journey along the east coast. The ship that he sailed
upon reached as far as Sofala, near the port of Beira in modern
Mozambique.

Masudi's observations are thought by some to lack accuracy; but if that is the case, they amply make up for it in description of details. He sketches a picture of traditional African

100

societies on the brink of becoming full-fledged states. He sub-stantiates their preference for iron with the comment:

"They wear iron instead of gold and silver."

He confirms that they produced "gold in abundance and other marvels"...that the climate was warm and the soil fertile... that the Zanj (the people of the coast) "use the ox as a beast of burden, for their country has no horses or mules or camels and they do not even know these animals." Masudi is not clear in his writings as to whether all or only some of the coastal inhabitants were blacks. It is a large country, he reports, and "is divided by valleys, mountains, stony deserts; (it) abounds in wild ele-phants but there is not so much as a single tame elephant."

Hunting elephants and gathering ivory are two other means of existence, Masudi observes, but they "make no use of ivory for their own domestic purposes." Instead, it was exported. African ivory has a special ritual significance in the Hindu marriage cere-mony; hence, the brisk ivory trade with India. Apparently only the softer ivory of East Africa has the qualities that enable the Indian craftsmen to work it to their own design and purposes. India is still one of the world's largest importers of ivory, and about half of the supply is used for making the traditional bangles for Hindu brides. Indians also use ivory for the hilts of swords and daggers and for fashioning chessmen.

In China, Masudi says, African ivory was put to a com-pletely different and even more spectacular use. Great and splen-did chairs were made for kings and high civil and military of-ficials, all of whom were carried on these portable thrones.

"No officer or notable dares to come into the royal pres-ence in an iron chair, and ivory alone can be used," Masudi asserts.

Sometimes tusks weighing up to 50 pounds were sent to China, he adds.

East African kings, Masudi continues, were called "wak-limi," which means "supreme Lord." The king of these Bantu peoples "has been chosen to govern them with equity," he adds. However, he remarks, "once he becomes tyrannical and departs from the rules of justice, they cause him to die" and other members of his family cannot succeed him. Masudi also observes that although these people "have no code of religion," they seem to be known for their orators, who "speak elegantly."

Some 200 years after the death of Masudi, Edrisi added to the knowledge of the east coast in his writings, done in 1154 at the behest of a Norman king of Sicily. Although much of Edrisi's work is hearsay, it is elaborate and detailed and includes charts and sketches. It depicts the enlargement and growing prosperity of the trading coast. Trade was based on iron, a catalyst for growth, he wrote. He characterized Malindi as the "city of the Zanj." The inhabitants were the mine workers, he said. Mombasa is mentioned by Edrisi as a contact port of the coast for the peoples of the interior.

As others have observed, Edrisi noted that iron was of more economic importance to the coastal peoples than gold. Remarking on its quality, he added:

"The iron of Sofala is known to be much better than the iron of India."

He asserted that trade was fairly well developed in this iron-dominated coastal economy of the 12th century. And like the Sahara Desert, the Indian Ocean was influential as a source and resource for not only tangible products but productions of the mind.

In exchange for the goods they exported, the peoples of the coast bought a myriad of commodities and luxury items. The coastal strip is littered with the fragments of these precious cargoes, whose presence also emphasizes the prosperity of the East African ports. Cloth and beads came from India. From China came ships laden with precious pottery and Ming porcelain in brown, green, gray, blue and white. Siam sent stoneware. Trade from the 12th century to the Portuguese arrival in the 15th century must have taken on dimensions unknown to the rest of the world.

Nine years before Vasco da Gama, Bartholomew Dias rounded the Cape of Good Hope, but fear of the unknown caused him to turn back. In December, 1497, Da Gama quelled the fears of his crewmen, bravely rounded the Cape and sailed into the Indian Ocean. He was a stubborn man and was determined to reach India. The adventure indeed turned out to be a brilliant one, for he stumbled upon the East African coast's city-states, which by then had developed into truly urban polities. Towns with tall, multistoried buildings in coral and stone glinted in the sun. Ships from the countries of the Far East filled the harbors. Under these sophisticated circumstances, the coastal peoples were hardly surprised to see yet other strangers entering their ports.

Da Gama's diary mirrors his first encounter with the inhabitants:

"When we had been two or three days, two gentlemen of the country came to see us. They were haughty and valued nothing that we gave them."

But for their part, the Portuguese "cried with joy," for here was the stuff of the adventurer's stories, songs and dreams. So, too, Durate Barbosa in 1500 found the whole aspect of the coast, its trade and its peoples new and astonishing. He immediately recognized the potentialities, for he had already witnessed the prosperity of the Indian Kingdom of Cambay, whose citizens had been made rich by the profits of the African coastal trade. It became the goal of both Barbosa and Da Gama to take charge of these profits and to make them their own.

Even after the Portuguese intrusion, the coastal city-states of Kilwa in the south and Pemba and Mombasa in the north did not band together as one unit to protect their interests against the Europeans. Nevertheless, they had a keen eye for keeping command of what was theirs, since rivalry among the sister-states was sharp. They therefore applied very restrictive tariffs against traders. The King of Mombasa imposed ferocious import rates. In the pre-conquest interlude, for example, he extracted a mitqal of gold, equal at the time to one-eighth of an ounce avoirdupòis, for each thousand lengths of cotton stuff imported into Mombasa. Kilwa was equally strict in applying protectionist rules along her southern stretch of coast. In Sofala, a merchant had to pay one length of cotton for every seven lengths sold to the king's agents.

Even when these "city-empires" were openly attacked by the Portuguese, there was no mechanism or tradition for banding together for the common defense. The links of these Swahili cities were the bonds of those engaged in a common-purpose trade. Both as a language and a culture, Swahili is rooted in Bantu. Linguistically, it differs from other Bantu languages in that it has a host of words borrowed from Arabic, Portuguese, Turkish, Malay, Persian, German and English. The foreign words have been tailored to accommodate African speech patterns. The poetry of the later Swahili writers in the 17th and 18th centuries is famous and useful for its insight into everyday life in those early times.

The coastal peoples' lack of political unity and competitive weapons resulted in their falling easy prey to the ferocity of the Portuguese. The intention of the foreign invaders was to use the coastal towns as bases from which they could attack other lands lying further to the east. Mozambique was the first city to be attacked. Then, in 1500, Kilwa was forced to pay tribute to the Portuguese king. The "events of Mozambique and Malindi" had put fear into the hearts of the people of Kilwa, according to a report by Vasco da Gama.

One of the largest fleets ever to sail to India was commanded by Francisco de Almeida, later to become Portugal's first viceroy in India. As Almeida's fleet bore down on Kilwa, a foreigner aboard--variously identified as a German or a Hollander--gave this eyewitness account:

"Many strong houses several storeys high" were plucked without opposition from the shocked inhabitants. He continued:

"The Vicar-General and some of the Franciscan fathers came ashore carrying two crosses in procession and singing... They went to the palace, and there the cross was put down and the Admiral prayed. Then everyone started to plunder the town of all its merchandise and provisions."

Dishonored by the Portuguese imposition of their tribute demand, the Sultan of Kilwa put his pain poetically when he said:

"It is better to be a jackal at large than a greyhound bound with a golden leash."

The sultan would have fled had he known what further humiliation was in store for his people. Although for a time he refused the Portuguese the rich jewels or the fixed sum of money that they demanded (for they knew of his power in the area), the sultan eventually was obliged to pay tribute in order to save his city. The action was no more than a respite, for eventually Kilwa was demolished.

Barbosa wrote in his impressions of Mombasa in the 16th century that the city was "very large and beautiful, and built of high and handsome houses of stone and whitewash, and with very good streets..." He continued:

"It has its own king, himself a Moor. The people are of dusky white and brown complexions; likewise, the women, who are bravely attired in silk and gold in abundance. It is a town of great trade and has a good harbor, where there are always many ships..., those which set sail for Sofala and those that come from

Cambay in India and Malindi and others which sail to the islands of Zanzibar, Mafia and Pemba...This Mombaça (Mombasa) is a country well supplied with plenty of food. Here are found very fine sheep, which have round tails, and many cows, chickens and very large goats, much rice and millet and plenty of oranges, sweet and bitter, and lemons, limes, pomegranates, Indian figs and all sorts of vegetables, and very good water."

Mombasa was destroyed and its people massacred by the Portuguese. Fortifications such as Fort Jesus were built at Mombasa by the invaders to house the garrisons which were necessary to control the local population.

These invaders from Portugal tried deliberately to disorganize the former trade routes, but they were wholly unsuccessful. Their aim was to change the established trade pattern to benefit their own towns, which they had firmly established in the south. Their ships sailed from Goa, a Portuguese enclave in India until modern times, to Malindi, Kilwa and the other East African ports. They never could comprehend that while the Arab traders lived on the coast, they were positively dependent on the caravans which were sent to bring out the supplies of gold, ivory and other exportable goods produced in the interior. That being the case, the good will of the interior's inhabitants was essential to this commerce. The Arabs had artfully and with great business acumen built up their political and commercial connections and correctly regarded them as two sides of the same coin. The Portuguese used the towns of the coast for organizing trade rather than as entrepots. Hence, having nothing to export and having no contact with the interior supplies of coveted raw materials, the coastal cities began to decline. Political and social deterioration followed, and the towns grew poorer and poorer until finally the African people began to attack them.

Poverty and misfortune never weakened the Swahili culture. After the Portuguese presence was eclipsed in the 17th and 18th centuries, the local kings continued to hold sway over the humbled coastal cities. It was their tradition to continue to reign. But as time went on, the real power seems to have shifted to a class of aristocrats, more loosely knit than the former royal power. The aristocracy no doubt consisted of the affluent who, among other things, supported the poets who flowered and proliferated in the 17th and 18th centuries. These poets, too, added to the east coast's historical record, for they described not only the customs of their own time but of days gone by. A lengthy religious poem called "Al-Inkishafi" gives us a picture of the lost towns. One sings of the diminished glory of Pate:

> "The cockroach whirring flits the empty halls;
> "Where nobles gathered, shrill the cricket calls."

The history of the coastal area falls within five periods, according to Moslem historians. The first could be described as the Times of Ignorance--roughly before the birth of Mohammed but also extending beyond the Prophet's time. The second was a medieval period during which the city-states flourished. The third was a Portuguese interlude in which a struggle for Swahili independence slowly grew and matured, eventually overlapping with a Swahili period that culminated in the long reign of Sayyid Said of Oman and Zanzibar (1840-1856). And finally, the fourth coastal period was marked by the conquest, division and administration by 19th century European powers.

It must be borne in mind that there is little consecutive history available to scholars even today. Excavations are sparse; and relatively little has been done in Kenya, Tanzania, Zanzibar or Pemba. But there are still inhabitants of the Kilwa area today who claim descent from the medieval sultans and who remember that the Royal Horn, symbol of authority, was thrown into the sea when the Germans arrived in East Africa. The last recorded person to have spoken with a member of the waning royal family of Kilwa was Captain Beaver of the frigate Nisus in 1811.

The poetry of the coast, called Swahili poetry, must be mentioned in order to evoke the aura and texture of coastal life;

for it is the heritage of the people who still dwell there. The known poetic centers were Lamu, Mombasa, Pemba, Zanzibar, Dar-es-Salaam and Kilwa. Although there were many dialects, there was always a free exchange of manuscripts. The old tradition was to write in Arabic characters and to end with the date and the words:

"Written with God's help by the poor, destitute and ignorant Fulani bin Fulani."

Those who wrote did so for the love of God; poverty was very much in line with their artistic principles. The form of Swahili-Arabic writing now in use in Mombasa is based on the Urdu variety of the Arabic script. The birth date of Swahili poetry is not really known. It is thought that it goes back to 1500 and may even have flourished earlier. But no extensive literature appears until the 16th, 17th and 18th centuries. Coastal poetry is generally believed to have been born at Pate, where many manuscripts belonging to the 18th century have been found. The poems "Hamziya," "Herekali" and "Inkishafi" all display a high degree of artistic competence. They could only have been written by those who had experienced a long literary tradition.

In all Swahili poetry, every line must have the same number of syllables. It is not permitted to insert lines of different lengths, as is done in European poetry. One of the most celebrated of poets is Muyaka bin Jaji al-Ghassaniy (1753-1837), whose works were collected by the Reverend W. E. Taylor in the 1890's under the title, "Diwani". Here is a sample from the poet's works:

"I was thinking deeply in my heart, here in
    this heart of mine,
"About all the things of this world; the one
    actor is God.
"As the time rolls by, so the things of this
    world revolve:
"Dust will become pots, pots will become
    dust."

An epic poem, one of the longest written in Swahili, was penned by the greatest author in the Swahili language, Shaaban Robert (1911-1962). It relates in 3,000 stanzas the history of the Second World War. Robert rose above the narrow approach to life, unlike many Moslem and Christian writers. As a result, he appeals to the modern mind in his search for new approaches to thinking in a more humane way.

CHAPTER 10 ANGLO-AMERICAN INTERREGNUM

The Anglo-Saxon age of African exploration dawned relatively late in history--at a time when the continent was emerging from the status of a curiosity into that of a Western European empire. Among the most influential men of this period were Dr. David Livingstone, Henry Morton Stanley, Richard Burton and Joseph Thomson.

DAVID LIVINGSTONE

Livingstone is a name familiar even to those totally ignorant of black Africa's past glories and with no more than a rudimentary knowledge of its modern transformation into a checkerboard of independent nations.

However, the passage of time has distorted much of the accomplishment and character of this most famous British explorer of the 19th century.

Actually, Livingstone was a crusader bent on redeeming the "Dark Continent"--whether or not it wanted redemption. Driven, as he insisted, by a "Great Power, " he was determined to assure the triumph of Christianity among what he considered to be pagan peoples. Yet because of certain personality defects, he was not entirely suited to the mission which he had set out to accomplish.

After landing at Cape Town from England, Livingstone arrived at Kuruman in southern Africa in 1841 in the service of the London Missionary Society. At the age of 27, his outlook was firm. He had a mission, and it bore the stamp of his personality. Whatever his shortcomings, he quickly discovered in the search to fulfill his mission that he had a taste for, and even delighted in, difficult travel. As he boasted in 1848, he could "bear what other Europeans would consider hunger and thirst without any inconvenience.

In 1848, propelled largely by sheer missionary zeal, he crossed the bleak Kalahari Desert, which he had heard was a populous territory watered by rivers.

That year, accompanied by William Cotton Oswell, an English missionary, he discovered Lake Ngami, a 20,000-square-mile body of water which he described as an inland sea. The discovery marked Livingstone's first triumphant step in Africa and in 1850 led to a grant by the Royal Geographical Society, which later published many of his writings.

The year 1852 found Livingstone back in Cape Town preparing to embark on what was heralded as his greatest achievement--a fearsome trek from Cape Town to Angola on the Atlantic and on across the continent to the central coast of Mozambique on the Indian Ocean.

The trans-African odyssey began at Cape Town in 1853. Livingstone traveled northward by way of Kuruman to Linyanti on the northern frontier of Bechuanaland and on into the country of the Kololo people. It was the Kololo chief, Sekeketu, who guided Livingstone to the discovery of the Zambezi River's awesome cataract which, in tribute to his queen, the explorer named Victoria Falls.

From the upper Zambezi, he struck westward into Portuguese Angola, where in 1854 he reached the Atlantic at the colony's capital, Luanda.

Then, in an about-face, he thrust eastward on a march that took him back to Linyanti and ultimately across the breadth of the continent. In May of 1856, he reached the Indian Ocean port of Quelimane in Portuguese Mozambique. Livingstone had completed a journey almost unparalleled in the history of African exploration.

Added to the natural hardships that confronted his party was the hostility of the Afrikaners, the Dutch colonists of South

Africa. Repeatedly, his column came under assault from the settlers, who ferociously attacked the African bearers with an animosity that they hold to this day. Once, they destroyed a house, at the expedition's base camp at Kolobeng.

News of the expedition created enormous interest in the outside world, nor was the public the only element to respond to the adventure. Cartographers, geographers and other specialists manifested keen professional interest as the explorer's accounts trickled back to London and seeped throughout the world. Missionaries immediately realized the Christianizing potential of the journey, for it opened new and useful territories for them and gave valuable clues to routes along which they could carry out their work. Many were horrified by Livingstone's tales of the slave trade, which had been tearing the fabric of life in the continent's interior.

Those with a commercial turn of mind were stirred by the possibilities for opening new markets for their goods. They were even able to rationalize their trade ambitions as a "civilizing mission" by applying the philosophy expounded by Livingstone, who said:

"No permanent elevation of people can be effected without commerce."

His own commercial success seemed to be assured when his "Missionary Travels and Researches in South Africa" was published. The book quickly captured the reading public's imagination at the unrivaled account of travel and adventure in Africa. It sold more than half a million copies. As a result of the book, its author became a national hero.

Yet favored as he was by fame and fortune, Livingstone remained a simple and even prosaic personality. He clung tenaciously to the belief that his travels were divinely inspired. It was characteristic of his attitude that he should have commented:

"I will not attribute any of the public attention which has been awakened to my own wisdom or ability."

At about this time, the British Foreign Office had taken an interest in opening a route from the mouth of the Zambezi River into the interior--a route which could freely and safely accomodate both commerce and missionaries. The two were considered to be interconnected and inseparable. The Foreign Office therefore supported Livingstone's second exploration project, which was to be based on the knowledge he had accumulated during his travels from 1853 to 1856.

Although his missionary zeal remained intact, he was no longer under the sponsorship of the London Missionary Society. One reason that he and the society parted company was that it had questioned whether his travels contributed meaningfully to what it considered to be the main purpose: spreading the Gospel.

For the new exploration, Livingstone's plan was to pass as quickly as possible through what was considered to be the unhealthy east coastal region of the Zambezi and to establish an up-river post in the Portuguese-held Tete region. He would also investigate the river's Kebrabasa rapids, an area he had never before visited, to determine if vessels could pass the treacherous stretch when the river ran high. Finally, he would establish a vital "civilizing center" as a jumping-off point for further exploratory expeditions.

Livingstone was to be accompanied by six Europeans, including his brother, Charles, and Richard Thornton, Norman Bedingfield and John Kirk. But Livingstone had a personality trait that made it difficult for him to lead or even communicate effectively with his staff--a defect which hampered the expedition. Indeed, the strain between him and his colleagues grew so great that he had to dismiss some of his British staff.

Nevertheless, he pushed on upstream until, finding the Zambezi impossible to follow, he paddled up the Shiré River, reaching Lake Nyasa in 1859 near the present independent republic of Malawi. There is little doubt that he can be credited with opening this region to future colonists.

He had already found that the Zambezi was unnavigable and, after exploring the Ruvuma, one of its major branches, came to the same conclusion about the tributary, which he reported would be of no use in penetrating the interior of Africa. These negative findings were in themselves substantial contributions to knowledge of the unchartered region. But ironically, that fact was unappreciated by the Foreign Office, which recalled the expedition in 1863 on the grounds that, since the Zambezi was unnavigable, further exploration would be useless. It was a bitter blow to Livingstone.

Back in England, he dedicated himself to satisfying an eager public's interest in his adventures along the Zambezi. Among other things, the journey yielded another Livingstone book: "Narrative of an Expedition to the Zambezi and its Tributaries." But literary endeavors, however successful, were not enough to satisfy his restless spirit. His acute sense of mission was too strong to permit him to remain comfortably in England.

At the suggestion of a wealthy and influential friend, Sir Robert Murchison of the Royal Geographical Society, he decided to set out on a search for the ultimate source of the Nile. He agreed to broaden the undertaking by making a general exploration of the Central African watershed--a region still known only imperfectly in spite of earlier expeditions by Richard F. Burton, John H. Speke and Samuel W. Baker. Again Livingstone was supported by the Foreign Office, which--as he had for his Zambezi expedition--once more awarded him consular rank.

In 1866 he set out on an expedition which proved to be the most significant journey of exploration undertaken by a European

in the 19th century. As a result of the expedition, European attitudes were moulded along rigid lines that profoundly influenced
the outlook and involvement of colonial powers on the African
continent for generations to come.

To avoid a repetition of the thorny relations between him
and his European subordinates on the previous expedition, Livingstone this time took Africans and Indians into his service as aides.

The column left the Tanganyika coast of East Africa at
Mikindani, north of the Ruvuma River, marched inland with the
aim of proving that a connection existed between Lake Nyasa and
Lake Tanganyika. But again his inability to lead plagued him.
Himself a man of immense stamina, he failed to make allowances
for the suffering that the difficult trek imposed on his followers.
His Indian subordinates deserted. Buffalo and camels brought
along to test their usefulness died under the assault of tsetse flies--
a loss which Livingstone blamed on the defected Indians, who had
been hired expressly to care for the herds. The expedition suffered another setback when a group of porters from the Comoro
Islands fled because of their fear of the Ngoni (Nguni) raiders.

At this crucial point, one of Livingstone's African bearers
deserted, taking with him the meager stock of medical supplies.

"I felt as if I had now received the sentence of death,"
Livingstone wrote later. Yet despite a constitution weakened by
previous expeditions, he struggled ahead without the medical supplies in the face of maleria, dysentery and other tropical health
hazards.

Undeniably, Livingstone's enormous stamina was matched
by his great personal courage. But there was another element
that doubtless contributed to the almost reckless fearlessness
which he displayed. Until his time, few Europeans in Africa had
been killed by black Africans. The white man on the Dark Continent still enjoyed relative immunity from personal assault.

Nevertheless, as Livingstone pushed on, he found it expedient to detour around Lake Nyasa to avoid hostile Arab slave traders who were active on the lake's northeastern shore. Continuing northward, he plunged deep into territory that was later to become part of the independent African state of Zambia. Here he paused at Lake Bangweulu before pushing on into the headwaters of the Congo River system. Eventually, at Lake Mweru, he marched into the eastern reaches of what is today the Democratic Republic of the Congo (Kinshasa, formerly Leopoldville).

But the gruelling trek was beginning to tell on the man whose personality combined elements of explorer, adventurer and missionary. Illness crippled him. Furthermore, his supplies were dwindling. Weak as he was, he struck out for the unknown territory west of Lake Tanganyika. He hoped to reprovision his expedition at Ujiji, an Arab port on the lake's northeastern shore. Bedevilled by poor health, he stumbled en route into Nyangwe, an Arab center on the east bank of the Congo. His mental state was such that he was uncertain whether the river was the Congo or the Nile. Suddenly, new castrophe struck: Arabs at Nyangwe massacred his African carriers.

All but broken in body and mind, he nevertheless succeeded in leading the remnants of his column to Ujiji.

It was at this time that Henry M. Stanley of the New York Herald dramatically arrived on the scene. As subsequent events were to prove, Stanley was a news reporter par excellence. He arrived with a caravan of supplies and a head full of questions. He sought and obtained one of the most courageous interviews in the annals of journalism: the story of the Livingstone expedition. Stanley's dispatches riveted the world's attention on both men and assured them a legendary place in history.

Stanley begged Livingstone to return to civilization, but the explorer refused. Instead, Stanley accompanied Livingstone

to the northern end of Lake Tanganyika to solve a nagging geographical problem: Whether the Ruzizi River flowed into or out
of the lake. Their investigation proved conclusively that the Ruzizi
poured its water into Lake Tanganyika.

Eventually, Stanley departed for Zanzibar, leaving his
extra supplies and bearers with Livingstone. Thus reprovisioned,
Livingstone was able to move again, this time southward to Lake
Bangweulu. Here, broken in health, he died in 1873. His body
was borne to the coast, from which it was shipped home to England.
Amid great ceremony, Livingstone was buried in Westminster
Abbey.

HENRY MORTON STANLEY

It is said by historians that the political exploration of
Africa followed in the footsteps of Henry M. Stanley.

The development probably was fortuitous. When the New
York Herald sent him to tropical Africa in 1871, it was solely to
find Livingstone.

For all the impact he was to have subsequently on the continent's development, it was ironical that Stanley should have insisted that he "detested the land most heartily" and that "I do not
think that I was made for an African explorer." He may have
been protesting too much, for the fact is, he made three important
explorations.

In 1874-1877, he crossed the continent from east to west.
Between 1879 and 1885, he worked for King Leopold II's International African Association in the Congo, later to become the Belgian Congo and now the Democratic Republic of the Congo (Kinshasa). And from 1887 to 1889, he commanded the Emin Pasha
Relief Expedition.

Hostile as he insisted he was toward Africa, there is more than a suspicion that he used his adventures to prove something about his own personality. Certainly that was the implication of those who criticized his style of exploration. One critic sneered that Stanley traveled across African soil in "martial array." Another accused him of adopting the practice of "making himself respected by dint of gunfire." And it was said frequently that he never traveled as a friend but as a belligerent.

Such accusations stemmed in part from jealousy. Many resented this upstart American journalist who, although his meeting with Livingstone undeniably quickened the pulse and pace of worldwide interest in Africa, was nevertheless suspected of appropriating and living in the reflected glory of the British explorer.

Yet there was more than a streak of truth in his detractors' charges. Stanley was outspoken and could be cruel, too. Richard Burton, the British explorer, once wrote indignantly to John Kirk:

"Of course, you have seen Stanley, who still shoots negroes as if they were monkeys."

Burton's harsh reference was based in part on a much-publicized event which happened during a boat journey down the western shore of Lake Victoria in 1875. With his supplies running low, Stanley tried to get provisions from the people of Bumbire Island. Their reluctance to accomodate him led to a fierce fight nearly disastrous to the Stanley expedition. The following June, while passing that way again, Stanley retaliated by attacking the islanders and inflicting heavy casualties. It was a prime example of the ruthlessness which often made his progress unnecessarily difficult.

It was also an act that was at variance with new ideas which were beginning to emerge in England about how the African continent should be approached. Thinking now revolved around the

white man's burden of responsibility and justice toward the Africans. Those who went out to the continent, this new philosophy
dictated, should be imbued with the humanitarian spirit.

Stanley was the antithesis of those who propounded these
sentiments. He could not be trusted to carry such lofty views in
his baggage as he swaggered across the continent. He clung stub-
bornly to the conviction that his methods--quite opposite from
those of Livingstone--were the best. More than once during his
travels with the journalist, Livingstone had had the greatest dif-
ficulty in preventing his companion from shooting down recalci-
trant Africans.

Stanley dismissed the charges against him with impatience.
He denied that his behavior was rash or his motives cruel. He
insisted that his aim, no less than that of Livingstone, was directed at the good of the Africans and that he and Livingstone dif-
fered only in method. Stanley asserted that in dealing with the
natives, Livingstone adopted an attitude that was almost Christ-
like and bordered on the foolhardy.

"The selfish and wooden-headed world requires mastering, as well as loving charity," Stanley said in his autobiography.

He had his supporters. Thomas H. Parke, a surgeon on
one of the expeditions, defended Stanley's disciplinary measures.

"To say that he was needlessly cruel or tyrannical is absolutely untrue," Parke wrote. "The beatings inflicted on the
carriers (which had evoked adverse comment from the Aborigines'
Protection Society of London) were only such as were absolutely
necessary to maintain the discipline on which the existence of the
expedition depended."

Stanley was able to boast financial backing which was enormous in comparison with that of other explorers. This very fact
put him under special obligation to his employers to complete his

expeditions with a dispatch that did not always leave time for the
amenities. As Sir Reginald Coupland wrote:

"Livingstone trudged across Africa. Stanley strode."

Between the two men, there was thus a difference in goal
and style. Stanley's expeditions, for example, were of awesome
size. In 1852, Livingstone had set out with 27 men, and in 1866
with 60. But Stanley started out on his 1874 march with 356 men
and, on the Emin Pasha Relief Expedition, embarked with an 804-
man entourage. While his other expeditions were smaller, the
complement nevertheless far exceeded the number which accompanied other African explorers.

Perhaps the speed with which he was required to carry out
his exploits suited his personality, for as he wrote:

"I have a most anxious temperament."

Stanley also had a great ability to organize. In fact, he
devoted an entire chapter in his book, "How I Found Livingstone
in Africa," to the technique of organization. This ability is the
key to understanding his accomplishments and was certainly in-
strumental in the success of the expeditions which later reaped
fame and reward for him.

For example, he made use of the knowledgeable Arab
merchants he met en route to find out as much as he could about
the tribal peoples he would encounter later on. From the Arabs,
he learned about tribal habits, preferences in trade goods which
might be most coveted by the Africans and other nuggets of information which might help to pave his way across the continent.

A clue to his organizational approach also can be seen in
a contract he drew up in 1874 for the porters whom he recruited
in Zanzibar. By the terms of the contract, the porters were given
a month's wages and rations from the day they enlisted. They

were required to abide scrupulously by the contract's terms, which included a clause which obliged them to perform their duties "cheerfully and promptly." For his part, Stanley agreed to treat the porters with kindness and to provide them with any necessary medication. He also agreed to judge disputes impartially and to protect them from attacks. Stanley never took these contracts lightly. On his return to Zanzibar at the close of the 1874-1877 expedition, he paid in full to their relatives the wages due those bearers who had died or been killed in his service.

On occasion, he was accused of having recruited slaves whose wages went into the pockets of their Arab owners. While admitting that there were many in his party whose status he could not prove, he insisted that every recruit was compelled to swear before signing on that he was a free man. Stanley argued (and apparently convinced himself) that his men were indeed working for themselves. At most, he said, some of his bearers might be slaves in name only who accounted to their masters only at the end of Ramadan, when they traditionally called to pay their respects.

Undoubtedly, part of Stanley's reputation for being harsh resulted from the fact that he spent much of his time teaching his men what he called "the novel lesson of obedience." The first leg was always the difficult part of any journey. It was then that discipline had to be established and that he was called on to exercise the greatest forebearance. Desertions were always at their highest during the first days of an expedition. As Stanley wrote:

"The dark brothers--chafing, restless, ferociously impulsive, superstitiously timid, liable to furious demonstration, suspicious and unreasonable--must be forgiven seventy times seven until the period of probation is passed."

Necessary as he thought punishment to be, he was not without an element of compassion. As punishment, for example, he preferred irons to the whip. And in a passage reflecting his mixture of discipline, frustration and mercy, he wrote that he had great trouble taking charge of "so many people totally innocent of anything approaching manliness." But he added:

"I could not help forgiving and forgetting."

Doubtless he realized that his workers were, after all, an indispensible means to his personal glory. Indeed, he later admitted that the "poor ignorant children of Africa" were his heroes.

Although Stanley's records include copious details of African customs and manners, the accounts are not always accurate. His views were totally subjective, untrammeled by any real knowledge. He was self-centered, and his works reflect that fact. Thus, he glibly classified tribes as either fierce or docile, according to the reception he received upon coming in contact with them. He made no allowance for the fact that African reactions varied from place to place, depending on tribal customs and the treatment meted out to them by outsiders. For example, the hostility of some tribes which he encountered resulted from their confusing his expedition with a raiding party of slavers or ivory hunters. On occasion--as in 1877 in the upper Congo and, a decade later, in the equatorial rain forest--the expedition might find directed against it the hostility of whole regions plunged into ferment by other causes.

One puzzling aspect of Stanley's personal relations was that he always seemed uneasy in the company of his fellow whites. At the same time, he managed to gain the respect of some African chiefs. But if he could avoid it, he never permitted his European assistants to establish friendly relations with Africans.

For practical purposes, he maintained close relations with Arab traders, including those who trafficked in "black ivory." In fact, in the early stage of his exploration, he seemed undisturbed by the slave caravans which crossed his path from time to time: he seemed to regard them as no more than a part of the exotic landscape.

It is true that by the time Stanley set foot in Africa, the main centers of the slave trade had dwindled along the East Coast and had shifted to the west. In the east, the interest in slaving had been replaced by the ivory hunt. However, slavery still flourished in the interior, and Stanley's outlook underwent modification as he became more familiar with that region. Between the great lakes and the upper Congo and Lualaba Rivers, he admitted, his exploration graphically revealed to him the terrible effects of the slave trade on the local peoples. The experience awakened him to the need to relieve the Africans of the torment of fear which the ugly commerce poised over their daily lives. One of his recommended remedies was a ban on the sale of firearms, presumably on the theory that such a prohibition would deprive the slavers of the superiority which firearms gave them over Africans and their primitive weapons. More significant for the colonial period that was to follow, he expressed the conviction that the only salvation for Africa and the Africans lay in the active European involvement in the continent.

As time went on, his mind focused more and more on the advantages of a European role in Africa. Indeed, his second journey has been regarded as having had a significant influence on European colonialism. It is said that the expedition, from east to west, established the continent's pattern of partition among the colonial powers and--in the mid-20th century--posed difficulties of frontier demarcation for African territories emerging into independence.

It is odd that the man who refused to be guided by moral strictures laid down in London should finally have begun to see for himself beyond the purely geographic contributions of his work, as happened when he recognized the continent as a rich field for humanitarian endeavor. But even then, his views were moulded by the conviction that humanitarianism lay along the road of commerce.

"Africa, "he wrote to The Times, "is inhabited by millions of robust, courageous men. It is no cant or sentimentalism, it is an obvious dictate of ordinary prudence, to say that if we are to hold these men in such control as shall make Africa equal to any continent in servicableness to mankind at large, it is by moral superiority, first of all, that control must be won."

A necessary component of this development, he argued, was the introduction of Christianity. In his book "The Dark Continent, " he said:

"My experience and study of the pagan prove to me...that if the missionary can show the poor materialist that religion is allied with substantial benefits and improvement of his degraded condition, the task to which he is about to devote himself will be rendered comparatively easy."

Stanley once said in all seriousness that the Almighty had intended Africa to play a role in the cosmos other than that of a "nursery for birds and a storehouse for reptiles." He had in mind, of course, a continent under the tutelage of Europe for the benefit of both. However, the modern conception is totally different: Africa is to serve no interest but her own. Stanley's ultimate answer could only be European occupation. Although Stanley played a marginal role in the imperialist scramble for Africa, his careful work for King Leopold II in 1879-1885 in the Congo Basin enabled the Belgian monarch to establish his claim to the territory at the Berlin Conference of 1884-1885.

It is still difficult to evaluate Stanley's impact on Africa. But it can be easily seen that he was the prisoner of the attitudes of his times and a captive of ambitions and circumstances not always under his control.

RICHARD F. BURTON

Richard Burton, rogue turned orientalist, came to Africa only because his first love--the Arab world--had been closed to him by political developments. He had traveled through the heartland of Islam and was an infatuated admirer of the land, its people and their language. He once journeyed from Medina to Mecca disguised as an Afghan doctor. So resourceful was he at avoiding detection that he developed the ability not only to write but to sketch secretly beneath the folds of his burnous--the loose, flowing Arab robe which covers from neck to toes.

But his explorations in and about Mecca finally became impossible because of unsettled conditions in the region. It was at that point that he turned his considerable talents to the vast expanse of Africa which still remained to be explored by Europeans.

Like Livingstone and Stanley, Burton had a personality defect: an irrepressible tendency to belittle those with whom he came in contact. Because of his love for the Arabian homeland, its people had been spared his barbed tongue and pen. Yet as early as his days at Oxford, this trait had been prominent in his character; he had called the dons "queer things" and complained that their pronunciation of Greek and Latin was execrable. For all that, he was brilliant, high-spirited and a serious scholar.

All of these characteristics were honed sharp during his years in the Indian army. The experience was grist for his literary mill--an outpouring that was to continue as he moved from adventure to adventure. But also, he was dogged by his own cynicism, often delivered with great wit and a rapier thrust as deadly as the sword that he wielded so expertly. Yet there was a considerable body of opinion that agreed that his jeers and snobbishness tarnished his unquestionably significant accomplishments.

Once he had turned his back on Arabia and moved on to press his imprint into the soil of Africa, it was characteristic

of him that he should have chosen as his initial target the Ethiopian center of Harrar--which, he could boast, he was the first
white man to visit. Following up the challenge, he next selected
Somaliland, whose people were known to be inhospitable to outsiders. On his journey to Somaliland, he was accompanied by
three Indian Army officers: Lieutenants G. E. Herne, William
Stroyan and John Hanning Speke. Their ultimate goal was the
East African hinterland deep in the interior south of Somaliland,
and Speke actually did some inland reconnaissance. But before
the expedition was well under way, it was overtaken by disaster.
Somali tribesmen ambushed Burton's column. Stroyan was killed.
Burton, Herne and Speke were seriously wounded but managed to
escape. They returned to England to recuperate. The outbreak
of the Crimean War in 1854 prevented them from resuming the
expedition.

After completing his war service, Burton began planning
a highly ambitious undertaking: the first modern exploration by
a white man of the interior of East Africa. Interest in the region
had been awakened by a map drawn by three 19th century missionaries who had worked for the British Church Missionary Society
of Mombasa. The trio had traveled into the interior and recorded
on the map the snowy peaks of both Mount Kenya and Mount Kilimanjaro. In addition, they had recorded what they called an "inland sea," variously designated as the Sea of Ujiji and the Sea of
Tanganyika.

Burton was stimulated by this early geographic document.
He wanted to determine for himself the limits of this "inland sea."
Taking a two-year leave of absence from the Army, he applied
for and won support of the Royal Geographical Society and the
British Foreign Office. While the expedition was in the planning
stage, Burton renewed his contacts with Speke, who was putting
together an expedition to central Asia.

Whether Burton realized it or not, he and Speke were of a
contrasting character--a fact which made Speke a particular asset

to any expedition undertaken by the flamboyant Burton. Coming from a background of country houses and stability, Speke was a disciplined man and not the prima donna that Burton had always been. He also had the immense physical stamina required for the challenge that lay ahead. Speke became the expedition's official surveyor; Burton was to concentrate on ethnographic studies and the commercial potential of the African interior.

Near the close of 1856, Burton and Speke reached Zanzibar. It will be recalled that at this period, the Portuguese already had lost their hold on East Africa's coast. The trading empire, which stretched from Zanzibar deep into the heart of Africa, was in the grip of Arabs. They had established an intricate commercial network dotted with inland stations to service the caravans that constantly and profitably moved through the region.

Burton was perceptive enough to realize that the Arab traders would do everything in their power to protect their investments against external interference. Without their consent and cooperation, Burton realized, the expedition was unlikely to get far. Fortunately for him, the age of British imperialism had not yet dawned in East Africa, and therefore Burton's mission could be passed off convincingly for what it was: a purely geographical exploration.

The upshot was that he solicited and obtained the sultan's invaluable assistance. Not only did the sultan arm Burton with letters of introduction to his people in the interior but he provided the exploration party with a caravan guide and, as an armed escort, a detachment of Baluchi mercenaries.

But the Burton expedition did not strike out immediately. First, it sailed to Zanzibar's neighboring island of Pemba. From there, it coasted northward to Mombasa and then southward to Pangani, on the African coast opposite Pemba. This desultory beginning was thought to be a kind of educated dallying, probably to avoid the season's torrential rains in the interior. Whatever the explanation, Burton made good use of the interlude. Although the expedition hadn't even got seriously under way, his facile pen was busy recording material which subsequently appeared in two volumes of travel.

Finally, at Kaole, on the coast opposite Zanzibar, Burton assembled his caravan. He quickly discovered that penetrating into the interior was going to be no easy task and that, more immediately, it was very difficult for a European to recruit porters. There was no prospect of signing on the 175 bearers he had expected to hire. At most, he managed to accumulate a crew of 35 men. Many of them were the personal slaves of merchants, who themselves were interested in slave-hunting and used the expedition as a means of doing a bit of surreptitious scouting for that human commodity. Two Goans were recruited as gun-carriers for Burton and Speke. One of them, Sidi Bombay, developed a lifelong interest in geography as a result of the expedition. Later, he played a valuable role in accompanying Speke on the expedition which pinpointed the source of the Nile in 1858.

Besides provisions and currency, Burton's caravan had to carry enough trade cloth and beads to last 18 months. His expert management of the ungainly cargo contributed in no small part to the success of the expedition. Management of personnel was at least as challenging. Burton said later in his writings that the Arab was too pampered for the back-breaking work involved and that the Swahili, whom he considered to be generally inferior, were really the best workmen. Of the caravan, he wrote:

"By dint of promises and threats, of gentleness and violence, of soft words and hard words, occasionally combined with the smart application of the bakur--the local 'cat'--by sitting in the sun, in fact, by incessant worry and fidget from 6 A.M. to 3 P.M., the sluggish, unwieldy body acquired some momentum."

Actually, Speke played a much more crucial role in the caravan's daily movement than Burton did. But Speke, modest and tactful, lacked Burton's great literary flair and so received little of the credit that was his due.

During the next 134 days, the caravan slogged through swamps, toiled across deserts and climbed over mountains. Illness dogged the expedition. What Burton recorded as "marsh fever" was particularly debilitating to the men; the victims had to be dragged up cliffs by those lucky enough to escape the plague that decimated the ranks.

There is no African recollection of what the indigenous peoples thought of the passing of the European expedition through their territory, but Burton--his thirst for knowledge insatiable and his pen constantly in motion--withheld nothing in detailing his travels. Often, he recorded that he and his men were stared at so unrelievedly that they felt as though they were in a menagerie.

The good offices of the sultan of Zanzibar proved useful to the caravan on more than one occasion. For example, at the Arab settlement of Kazeh, the Tabora of today, Burton was received hospitably by Snay bin Amir, an important and knowledgeable man. Snay bin Amir was responsible for pointing the direction to the rumored "great lake," which the Arabs called the Sea of Ukerewe or the Sea of Nyanza, to the north. He suggested that Burton visit this "inland sea" instead of continuing with his plan to reach Lake Tanganyika, but Burton decided to keep to his original itinerary. The English explorer was convinced that Lake Tanganyika would prove to be the Nile's fountainhead, the discovery of which was the declared aim of his expedition.

At last, on February 19, 1858, Burton's eyes for the first time swept over the vast expanse of Lake Tanganyika. Both he and Speke were ill when they reached their goal. Speke was suffering from an eye inflammation caused by a prolonged bout with malaria. The same disease had partially paralyzed Burton. In spite of his physical condition, Burton remained intent on push-ing ahead to explore a large river which reportedly flowed at the lake's northern end. On the basis of vague rumors, the river was designated as the Ruzizi, but no European had seen it. Some-what recovered from the malaria attack, Speke tried in vain to hire a dhow from an Arab who related that he had sailed the north end of Lake Tanganyika and was familiar with the Ruzizi. The river, the Arab sailor declared with a great show of authority, flowed out of the lake and not into it. Burton was overjoyed at the news; it dovetailed with his speculation that the Ruzizi was the ultimate headwater of the Nile.

But Speke was skeptical of the accuracy of the Arab's in-formation. He himself estimated the altitude of Lake Tanganyika at 1,800 feet--too low to be the source of the Nile, considering that the East African plateau's average elevation was probably twice that great. The disagreement strained relations between the two Englishmen.

Eventually, the explorers managed to rent a dhow and sail northward, Speke almost deaf from a beetle which had lodged painfully in his ear. The discovery that awaited them at the north-ern end of the lake was not one to improve the contentious Burton's frame of mind. Investigation proved conclusively that he had been wrong and that Speke had guessed correctly; the Ruzizi River did, indeed, flow into Lake Tanganyika, itself sunk in a narrow trough of volcanic origin. The Nile's source still eluded Burton.

Embittered toward the man with whom he had endured so much hardship, Burton led the expedition back to Ujiji, where fresh supplies were to have been awaiting him. However, the expected baggage had not arrived, and his plan to explore southward was frustrated. Actually, Burton had already completed the assign-ment entrusted to him by the Foreign Office. He had been able to determine the configuration of Lake Tanganyika, either by di-rect observation or by interviews with knowledgeable informants. Furthermore, he had been successful in gathering detailed in-formation about the commerce and peoples in the area.

After a month's journey eastward from Ujiji to Kazeh, Speke left Burton to rest and to amass whatever new material he could in the immediate environs. Speke himself went off on a new exploratory trip, guided principally by his instinct. On August 25, 1858, he returned exalted to announce "the startling fact" that he had discovered the sources of the White Nile.

Burton was taken aback. Speke, he had to admit, was a man of immense experience in the field of exploration. Nevertheless, Burton greeted his countryman's painstaking accumulated evidence with his customary derision. A quarrel broke out. Friendship quickly turned into bitter enmity, largely through Burton's inability to curb his disposition to belittle anyone who seemed to threaten his own pre-eminence. Later, he wrote slightingly of Speke's exploit:

"The fortunate discoverer's conviction was strong; his reasons were weak."

He referred to Speke's triumph--one of the greatest in the region's history--as a "pretended discovery." Burton's disposition to jeer, amounting almost to an automatic reflex, cost him whatever share he might have claimed for discovering the Nile's headwaters.

While Burton went on to Kilwa on Tanganyika's Indian Ocean, Speke headed back to London, where the Royal Geographic Society asked him to report on his findings. At first, he was reluctant to accept the invitation, fearing that it would seem unfair to absent Burton. But he was persuaded. Speke's presentation, bolstered by painstaking evidence and sound reasoning, convinced the society's members that he had, indeed found the long-sought source of the Nile.

To Burton's credit, it must be admitted that when he appeared on the same platform to receive a Royal Geographical Society gold medal, he did not try to depreciate his companion's accomplishments. But there is little doubt that Burton continued to smoulder with envy. He had always considered the exploration of East Africa to be solely in his hands--a conceit of which he was disabused when Speke published his own journal of the expedition. To Burton, the trip had been a failure, and he continued to heap scorn on his rival and his Nile theory long after Speke's accidental death.

Burton's own work was a vivid description of not only the topography but the ethnography of the region he had crisscrossed. And in his depiction of the interior's inhabitants, he exercised the same vituperation which he had earlier leveled at Speke. He spared neither the Africans nor the Arabs. He observed caustically that the slave trade had failed to civilize the Africans, whom he consigned to a limbo of inferiority. At the same time, in an allusion to the Arab slavers, he wrote that their brutal trade "practically annihilates every better feeling of human nature."

Although Burton's place in history is based on his pioneering East African exploration, he did more than dabble in West Africa. In 1860, he won a Foreign Office assignment to the island of Fernando Po, off Nigeria. Yet despite his fame, as well as his prominent social connections through his wife's family, he was able to capture nothing more elevated than a consular post at Fernando Po--hardly a challenging job for a man of his energy and literary luster.

Finding that his consular duties--then an ill-defined field of work--failed to satisfy his inexhaustible interests, Burton filled the gap with ethnographic exploration. He turned to the study of the west coastal Kingdom of Dahomey and produced works which, though now dated in outlook, nevertheless are still considered a landmark. Among other things, he was privileged to see the court of the Fon people at a time when it was still a living institution.

He found little time in those days to perform his official Foreign Office duties; and he was not always successful in fulfilling the missions assigned to him. For example, he never was able to abolish the slave trade nor did he succeed in ending the practice of human sacrifice that flourished in the ancient Kingdom of Dahomey. Such failures as plagued him may be attributable in part to his old shortcoming--an absence of tact--which had dogged him through most of his life.

Yet in his ethnographic dealings, he successfully brought to bear his unflagging interest and an almost intuitive understanding of the Dahomey kingdom's inner workings. He even managed to suppress in the writings covering this period his tendency to jeer and mock the people and their way of life. He had, after all, a firm grip on scholarship when he chose to exercise it. Like few others, he could etch the face of Africa through the facts he accumulated in both east and west. Whenever he was at his best, he was fair-minded and objective, contributing monumentally to the outside world's understanding of the continent and its peoples. At such times, his writings stand mountain-high above his less objective works. It was only when he diverged from the path of scholarship to mock and jeer that he performed a disservice to the Africa he loved.

For tragically, the uncritical have perpetuated many of Burton's less substantial conclusions, notably the myth of African "inferiority" and the "burden" which he was convinced devolved upon the white man as a result. Such attitudes die hard. They are expressed in many circles to this day.

JOSEPH THOMSON

British explorer Joseph Thomson wanted his epitaph to read:

"The last tramp--or how Thomson found the true spirit of Africa and pegged out his last claim on the Dark Continent."

The fascination of Africa was rooted early and deep in Thomson. As a youth, he had tried unsuccessfully to volunteer for the 1878 Livingstone relief expedition. His boyish exuberance also led him impulsively to make application for membership in a Royal Geographical Society expedition which, he had read in a brief newspaper item, was about to leave for Lake Nyasa.

He fancied himself a latter-day Livingstone--his hero from boyhood. He was certain that he was destined to become a gentle friend of "the noble savage" and a solver of geographic and scientific riddles. This spark of romanticism flared early and was never dimmed by age. In fact, he remarked two years before his death that he would die "with the spirit of Africa on my lips." Like his heroes--Stanley, Livingstone and Speke--Thomson loved mystery and drama, and his ego demanded the psychic rewards which flowed so naturally from success.

But because of his character, his methods were uniquely his own. Eschewing the swashbuckling approach, he proclaimed the motto:

"He who goes softly goes safely; he who goes safely goes far."

He later proved the soundness of this aphorism, which guided his behavior during his years of exploration. Throughout, his gentleness was in contrast to the unfeeling attitudes adopted by many of his countrymen who cared little whether they came to Africa as peaceful inquirers or as insolent conquerors. To the gentle Thomson, it mattered a great deal. The result was that he was able to carry out his explorations without invariably leaving behind a reservoir of hostility or resentment among those with whom he came in contact. It was an accomplishment of some dimensions for a man of his super-heroic times.

Between 1879 and 1891, Thomson remained in Africa, crisscrossing the continent's eastern regions on many-faceted journeys: geographic, diplomatic and commercial. His opportunity to realize his dream came when he was only 21 years of age. Keith Johnston Jr. had been selected to lead a Royal Geographical Society expedition from Dar es Salaam to Lake Nyasa and Lake Tanganyika. But at that crucial point, Johnston died and Thomson was chosen to serve in his place. It was the first opportunity for the young man, trained at the University of Edinburgh as a geologist, to take the reins of responsibility. Despite his youth and inexperience, he seems to have had no doubt that he was qualified to follow in the footsteps of his heroes.

In fairness, it must be admitted that Thomson's introductory expedition might well have been less successful, if not disastrous, without the invaluable assistance of James Chuma and Makatuba, two African guides attached to his retinue. It was they who led him safely through the country of the Mehenge and the Hehne peoples, who live at the northern end of Lake Nyasa. Burton, who had passed through the region 28 years before, hated the Hehne as a savage and inferior people. But Thomson, who never subscribed wholeheartedly to the racist views of earlier pioneers, was attracted to the Hehne. In a passage remarkable for his day, he wrote:

"Whatever might be the colour of our skin, there existed no barrier between us nor any difference but that of degree between our respective feelings and sentiments."

Burton had labeled the Hehne "determined pilferers." Ignoring Burton's character evaluation, Thomson left his camp unguarded and later had the satisfaction of being able to report:

"No one put forth his hand to touch what did not belong to him."

In Gilbertian terms, he found the Hehne "exceedingly polite" and thought it "only right to return the compliment."

As he matured, Thomson increasingly became interested
in the dark-skinned peoples among whom he moved. They had,
he learned, distinctive personalities; and with his insatiable curi-
ousity aroused, he set about making an intensive investigation of
their customs and manners. It was singularly broad-minded for
the times that he should have propounded the idea that it was unfair to judge peoples on the basis of the relatively short time
which Europeans had, until then, spent among the Africans. He
suggested further that the white man's caravans were by their
nature so intrusive that all reflections on the lives of the inhabitants were bound to be biased. And although he was to modify
his views somewhat at a later date, he concluded that Africans
had been unfairly caricatured.

He wrote that "under the influence of fevers and the thous-
and troubles attendant on African travelling," explorers as a
group had abused Africa's people in print.

"Few people," he added, "have studied them with unprejudiced and unbiased minds."

Even when he found occasion to express criticism of the
native style of dress or decoration, Thomson recognized that the
standards of attractiveness differ from culture to culture.

Thanks in large part to the expertise of his knowledgeable African guides, the expedition became the first commanded
by a European to cross the high plateau that separates Lake Nyasa
from Lake Tanganyika. It then proceeded half-way up the western shore of Tanganyika to the Lukuga River, where Thomson
was able to verify the existence of an outlet that governed the
lake's water level. He then followed the Lukuga westward, almost
to its confluence with the upper Congo.

At this point, the expedition encountered local hostility.
As a result, the caravan was forced to retrace its route. Arriving on the southeastern shore of Lake Tanganyika, Thomson

became the first European to catch sight of Lake Rukwa to the east. Marching northward to Kazeh (Tabora), the expedition then turned eastward and finally reached the Indian Ocean.

Thus ended in the late 1800's a 14-month trek which had taken Thomson more than 3,000 miles through territory imperfectly explored or totally unknown by Europeans. One result was that he was now able to supply the scientific community with the answers to old, nagging questions about the geological and geographic configuration of East Africa. It was a source of justified satisfaction to them that the expedition had returned safely and intact. There had been no heated arguments, no friction between Thomson and his men. And not a shot had been fired--a fact which spoke eloquently of his gentleness and tact in dealing with the inhabitants whom he encountered.

Thomson was rewarded by the praise that he deserved, but he modestly and justly gave their full share of credit to his guides, Chuma and Makatubu.

In 1882, Thomson again enlisted Chuma's services. This time the assignment was to take a small caravan up the Ruvuma and Lugenda Rivers, between the Indian Ocean and Lake Nyasa, to find coal or other mineral deposits for the sultan of Zanzibar. The search was in vain.

Thomson's most ambitious and geographically significant journey was taken between 1883 and 1884. The expedition's purpose was to explore and report on the region lying between Mount Kilimanjaro and Victoria Nyanza (Lake Victoria)--the last unopened territory of any significance in tropical Africa.

The land was occupied by the Masai, a reputedly hostile people who blocked the route into the untapped markets said to exist in the flourishing kingdom of Buganda (now part of the Republic of Uganda). Until Thomson's arrival, the Masai had refused to permit any European to advance into their territory beyond Kilimanjaro.

Thomson, a man of quiet courage, felt confident that his wits and determination were equal to theirs. But his first attempt to pierce their barricade failed. The Masai were, he discovered, as militant as reported. His caravan was forced to retreat. However, Thomson reorganized for a second attempt and, combining his party with a caravan of traders for additional strength, marched northward from Kilimanjaro through the Masai-occupied territory to the foot of Mount Kenya.

His unhampered penetration into the hostile land was accomplished more by his personal charm than by the show of strength. For he was attracted to the Masai more forcefully than he had been to the Hehne. The Masai, aristocratic in physique and independent in their nomadism, were untroubled by any feeling of inferiority. On the contrary, they carried themselves with a kind of arrogant pride. Their hostility to unwelcome strangers, backed as it was by unflinching courage, had heretofore kept explorers at a discreet distance. It was perhaps these traits that drew Thomson to the Masai. Romantic that he was, he admired what he regarded as the "noble savage" unspoiled by civilization and free in his unfettered nomadic life.

For their part, the Masai at least tolerated Thomson. He reported that they delighted in tormenting him in a spirit of rough good humor. They were insatiably curious about him, and he reported bearing many "humiliations" at their hands as they inquisitively stroked his skin and fingered his hair. Troublesome as they were, he would hear no criticism of them; and in time he compared all other Africans unfavorably with the Masai.

From Mount Kenya, the expedition moved on to establish the configuration of Lake Baringo, traversed the Uasin Gishu Plateau and reached Victoria Nyazna near the Kavirondo Gulf. Then, turning northward, Thomson led the caravan to the foothills of Mount Elgon.

By now, Thomson was debilitated by dysentery and the brutal pummeling of a 3,000-mile march through a wild and largely uncharted region. Yet his achievements had not passed unnoticed. Not only his contemporaries but generations to come would marvel at the accounts of his remarkable and scientifically enlightening adventures in the raw interior of East Africa.

Thomson was noteworthy throughout his travels for progressing through tact and diplomacy and rarely showing the flag of belligerence. Such peaceful means took more time and ingenuity than might otherwise have been required, but they had the virtue of leaving the face of Africa unscarred by lasting hostility.

During his early years on the continent, Thomson had been unstinting in his admiration of Africans. They could, it seemed, do no wrong. In contrast to his European predecessors, he did not consider them to occupy a lower order on the scale of the human race. He got on well with his porters, few of whom deserted. Chuma, Makatubu and others eagerly signed on for one expedition after another. The secret of Thomson's successful dealings with the Africans at this stage may have been that, because of his youth, he did not insist on the ritual obeisance that the older explorers had demanded.

But in the last years of his life, Thomson modified his views; they changed from admiration and affection to the more stereotyped attitudes of the day. Only the Masai remained undiminished in his mind. This change may have come about because, as he grew older, he became less romantic. Or it may have been that society forced him to conform to the prejudice of the day, for this was a time when he was trying to please a literary public with his writings. Perhaps, too, his wholehearted admiration was reserved for Africans still imbued with what he called "primitive virtues."

Whatever the explanation, his change of attitude seems to have coincided with the shock experienced on first encountering

West Africans. Certainly, his sensibilities were shaken by a trip to Sierra Leone. There, in Freetown, as well as at Lagos, Nigeria, he met Africans who took themselves seriously and were unabashed by European "superiority." West Coast Africans had always been considered more sophisticated than their eastern brothers.

What Thomson apparently found insupportable was the urbanization of the western Africans. Even then, they were making selective use of European influence for their own benefit. It was an early stirring of their determination to lift themselves out of the rural poverty, however much their "simple life" may have appealed to European romantics. The process, and the problems attending the metamorphosis, continues to this day.

Thomson detected this modernizing trend and disapprovingly contrasted it with the simplicity of the Masai. The jolting West African experience injected a sting of bigotry into his later literary works. Thus, he wrote:

"We have made the mistake of attempting to govern the negroes on lines utterly unsuited to their stage of development. If you can imagine what would be the result of acting with a boy of 10 as if he had the same rights and privileges of an adult--as if he was quite capable of taking a position among his elders on a footing of equality--you will have an idea of what sort of offensive creature our method of rule has made the West Coast negro." Thomson's attitude is familiar as the now-discredited "colonial mentality." He both mistrusted and feared Africans who adopted modern habits--who, in effect, sought to rise above "their place" as defined by Europeans. The peoples of the Niger brought out the worst in Thomson. He changed his views about the innate capacity of the dark-skinned peoples. He began to think that the European "civilizing mission" was doomed to failure in black Africa. In adopting this attitude he was, of course, ignorant of the continent's ancient empires.

Thomson seemed incapable of bringing to bear the gentleness and humanity of outlook of his early years. He began to
heap abuse on Africans, as Burton had. The West Africans, he
complained, were "spoiled" and pretentious. Such expressions
as "semi-civilized" crept into his vocabulary to designate the
peoples, whom he now regarded as objects devoid of all rational
behavior. Thus, his otherwise successful explorations lacked
depth and vision; and as he grew older, he unfortunately became
increasingly short-sighted. Despite this deterioration in tolerance,
Thomson's stature has grown as his exploits recede in time. It
may be that history has been kind to him, remembering his youth-
ful period and glossing over his intolerant older years.

During Thomson's lifetime, the classic age of exploration
already had passed into the imperial epoch which took its orien-
tation from the pioneering footsteps of Henry Morton Stanley.
By 1884, France had annexed parts of West Africa to its holdings
along the coast and rivers of Senegal and Guinea. The French
also occupied ports on the Slave Coast and stations on the Congo
and Ogooue Rivers. Even before, Stanley had claimed Kinshasa
on the south bank of the Congo for Belgium's King Leopold II. The
Germans had annexed Southwest Africa and made protectorates
of Togo and Kamerun (Cameroon).

Although Thomson disclaimed any contribution to the expansion of imperialism, his expeditions had an indirect if unin-
tentional effect in the period of active rivalry among the colonial
powers. Explorers and administrators who followed in his footsteps often testified to the fact that Thomson's enlightened dealings with the Africans made their own objectives easier to attain.
Henry Hamilton (later Sir Harry) Johnston, who climbed Kilimanjaro in 1884, paid tribute to the impression that Thomson had left
in the region. There had been travelers in Africa, Johnston said,
whose paths it would be disadvantageous to follow; but Thomson
was a rare exception because of "the excellent impression that he
had left behind among the natives." Johnston concluded:

"I never heard a single complaint with regard to the con-
duct of Mr. Thomson's expedition, though very few expeditions
would traverse so difficult a country without leaving some friction
behind."

GLOSSARY

ACROPOLIS--A group of buildings, often a citadel or fortress, constructed on high ground.

ANTIMONY--A chemical element. When powdered, it is widely used in the Arab world as an eye cosmetic.

ARTIFACT--An implement, weapon or other product of human workmanship, as opposed to an object formed by natural causes.

BARROW--A prehistoric burial mound.

BRONZE AGE--A period characterized by the use of bronze weapons or implements. The chronological period varies in different parts of the world, but it invariably forms an intermediate stage between the Neolithic Period (New Stone Age) and the Early Iron Age.

CAIRN--A heap of stones raised as a monument or landmark.

CTESIPHON--A capital of the Parthians, a semi-nomadic Iranian people who lived in the third century B.C. to the southeast of the Caspian Sea. Under Mithradates I, the capital was at Ctesiphon on the middle Tigris.

CURSIVE--A style of writing in which the characters are formed without raising the pen so that the separate strokes are joined. The angles of the characters are rounded and often slanted.

DENDROCHRONOLOGY--The study of the pattern of tree rings. These studies are based on the fact that the sequence of dry and wet seasons produces the same pattern of rings in all trees growing at the same time in the same place. However, dendrochronology is of no help at Zimbabwe because there are no trees within 20 miles of the site.

143

EARTHWORK--A general term describing any system of banks
or ditches raised for protective or ceremonial purposes in prehistoric times. The most simple earthwork is a ditch or a bank,
a natural or primitive form of defense.

ETHNOBOTANY--The study of the uses of plants by various peoples. The oldest area of cultivation will normally have the greatest number of varieties of any given plant.

HABITATION SITE--Any place in which traces of human occupation have been found, whether marked by human skeletons, artifacts, pottery fragments or other settlement indicators.

OLDUVAI GORGE--A canyon cut across the Serengeti Plain of
Tanzania. Formed from sediments laid down during the Pleistocene Epoch, it was carved 300 feet deep by the Olduvai River.
One of the world's principal palaeontological sites, the gorge con-
sists of strata of black volcanic basalt at the lowest level, topped
by a layer of bright red sediment over 100 feet thick. Above that
lies a stratum of gray sediment overburdened with recent steppe-
limestone, which forms the present ground surface.

PALAEONTOLOGY-- The study of extinct life forms generally
known only through fossils. This discipline crosses the path of
archaeology when artifacts are found in association with fossils.

PLUVIAL PERIOD--A time of heavy rainfall.

POTASSIUM-ARGON DATING--A scientific method of dating remains of the past. The technique depends on the known disintegration rate of the radioactive isotope, potassium-40, into argon-
40. It is used to date remains older than those which can be dated
by the radiocarbon method.

PREHISTORY--The period of man's evolution and development
before the invention of writing.

QUATERNARY PERIOD--A time span, the beginning of which dates back more than a million years. It has been divided into the Pleistocene Epoch, which carries up to the Holocene, beginning about 10,000 years ago and continuing to the present.

PUNT--Egyptian designation for the African coast south of Egypt. "The Land of Punt" was first mentioned on the Palermo Stone dating from the reign of Sahure in the fifth Egyptian dynasty.

PARKLAND--A level valley between mountain ranges.

RELICT--A persistent remnant of an otherwise extinct flora and fauna. Such organisms may leave a relief feature in stone after other parts have vanished.

TIGRINYA--A central Ethiopian people, mainly Christian but also including a few Moslems. About half of the estimated population of 1,150,000 lives in Eritrea. The Tigrinya economy rests on the cultivation of cereal grains.

WADI--The bed or valley of a stream. Except during the rainy season, when it may form an oasis, it is usually a sharply defined, dry gully.

BIBLIOGRAPHY

CHAPTER I

Brace, C. L., "The Origins of Man," Natural History Magazine, Vol. LXXIX, no. 1, 1970.

Butzer, Karl, Environment and Archaeology, Aldine Press, Chicago, 1964.

Clark, Graham, "World Prehistory," Cambridge University Press, 1969.

Clark, J. D., "Human Ecology during the Pleistocene and Later Times in Africa South of the Sahara," Current Anthropology, I, 1960.

Clark, J. D., "The Prehistoric Origin of African Culture," Journal of African History, Vol. V, 1964.

Clark, J. D., "The Spread of Food Production in Sub-Saharan Africa," Journal of African History, Vol. III, no. 2, 1962.

Gabel, Creighton, "Prehistoric Populations of Africa," Vol. 2, Boston University Press, 1966.

Leakey, L. S. B., "Exploring 1,750,000 Years in Man's Past," The National Geographic Magazine, Vol. 120, no. 4, Oct. 1961.

McCall, D. F., Africa in Time Perspective, Boston University Press, Boston, 1964.

Posnansky, Merrick (ed.), East African Vacation School--Prelude to East African History, British Institute of Archaeology, Nairobi, 1959.

Sahlins, Marshall D., "The Origins of Society," Scientific American, Vol. 203, no. 3, September, 1960.

Simpson, George Gaylord, Life of the Past, Yale University Press, 1953.

Singer, Charles (ed.), History of Technology, Vol. I, Oxford, 1953.

Thomas, W. L., (ed.), Man's Role in Changing the Face of the Earth, Chicago, 1958.

Washburn, Sherwood L., "Tools and Human Evolution," Scientific American, Vol. 203, no. 3, September, 1960.

Wrigley, Christopher, "Speculations on the Economic Prehistory of Africa," Journal of African History, Vol. 1, 1960.

CHAPTER II

Adams, William W., "An Introductory Classification of Meroitic Pottery," Kush, 1964.

Alimen, H., The Prehistory of Africa, Hutchinson, Scientific and Technical, London, 1957.

Arkell, Anthony J., Early Khartoum, Oxford University Press, London, 1949.

Arkell, Anthony J., A History of the Sudan from the Earliest Times to 1821, 2nd. ed., London, 1951.

Arkell, Anthony J., "The Sudan South of Khartoum," Report of a conference held in July, 1953 at School of Oriental and African Studies, London, 1955.

Cole, Sonia, The Prehistory of Africa, Mentor Books, New York, 1963.

Crowfoot, J. W., The Islands of Meroe, Oxford, 1911.

Davidson, Basil, The African Past, Little Brown and Company, Boston, 1964.

Davidson, Basil, Old Africa Rediscovered, Gollancz, London, 1960.

Davidson, Basil, Africa in History, Macmillan, 1968.

Emery, W. B., Archaic Egypt, Penguin, London, 1961.

Fage, J. D., A Short History of Africa, Oxford, London, 1962.

Guggenheim, Hans, "Smiths of the Sudan," Natural History Magazine, Vol. 70, no. 5, May, 1961.

Hintze, Fritz, "Preliminary Report of the Butana Expedition 1958," made by the Institute for Egyptology of the Humboldt University, Berlin, translated by Cicely Morgan, Kush, VII, 1959.

Hintze, Fritz, "Preliminary Report on the Excavations at Muswarat Es Sufra, 1960-1," Kush, 1962.

Keating, Rex, "The Changed Face of Nubia," U.N.E.S.C.O. Features, no. 549, April (II), 1969.

Littmann, E., "The Decline and Fall of Meroe," translated from the German by L. P. Kirwan, Kush, 1950.

McCall, Bennett, Butler (eds.), Eastern African History, Boston University Papers on Africa, Vol. III, Praeger Special Studies, 1969.

Murdock, G. P., Africa: Its Peoples and their Culture History, McGraw-Hill, 1959.

Shinnie, P. L., Meroe, A Civilization of the Sudan, Thames & Hudson, 1967.

Shinnie, P. L., "New Light on Medieval Nubia," Journal of African History, Vol. VI, no. 3, 1965.

Trigger, Bruce, History and Settlement in Lower Nubia, Yale University Publications in Anthropology, New Haven, 1965.

Wainwright, G. A., "Iron in the Napatan and Meroitic Ages," Sudan Notes and Records, XXVI, 1945.

CHAPTER III

Horvath, Ronald J., "The Wandering Capitals of Ethiopia," Journal of African History, Vol. X, no. 2, 1969.

McCall, D. F. (ed.), Eastern African History, Praeger, New York, 1969.

Simoons, Frederick J., Northwest Ethiopia: Peoples and Economy, University of Wisconsin Press, 1960.

Ullendorf, Edward, The Ethiopians, Oxford University Press, 1965.

CHAPTERS IV, V, VI

Fouché, Lee, Mapungubwe, Cambridge, 1937.

Fagan, Brian, "Early Trade and Raw Materials in South Central Africa," Journal of African History, Vol. II, no. 3, 1966.

Fagan, Brian, Southern Africa, Praeger, New York, 1965.

Jaffey, A. J. E., "A Reappraisal of the Rhodesian Iron Age up to the Fifteenth Century," Journal of African History, Vol. VII, no. 2, 1966.

Oliver, Roland, "The Problem of Bantu Expansion," Journal of African History, Vol. X, no. 1, 1969.

Posnansky, Merrick, "Pottery Types in East Africa," Journal of African History, Vol. II, no. 2, 1960.

Posnansky, Merrick, "Bantu-Genesis--Archaeological Reflections," Journal of African History, Vol. IX, no. 1, 1968.

Singer, Charles (ed.), History of Technology, Oxford, 1954.

Summers, Roger, Inyanga, Cambridge, 1958.

Summers, Roger, "The Southern Rhodesian Iron Age," Journal of African History, Vol. II, no. 1, 1961.

Vansina, J. (ed.), The Historian in Tropical Africa, The 4th International African Seminar, University of Dakar, 1961, Oxford, 1964.

Whitty, Anthony, "The Origins of the Stone Architecture of Zimbabwe," Proceedings of the Pan-African Congress on Prehistory, London, 1957.

Williams, J. G., The Birds of East and Central Africa, Houghton Mifflin Company, Boston, 1964.

CHAPTERS VII, VIII and IX

Bishop, W. D. (ed.), Background to Evolution in Africa, University of Chicago, Chicago & London, 1967.

Chittick, Neville, "The 'Shirazi' Colonization of East Africa," Journal of African History, Vol. V, 1964.

Chittick, Neville, "Kilwa and the Arab Settlement of the East African Coast," Vol. IV, no. 2, 1963.

Clark, J.D., "The Prehistoric Origin of African Culture," Journal of African History, Vol. V, 1964.

Freeman-Grenville, G. S. P., "East African Coin Finds and Their Historical Signifance," Journal of African History, Vol. I, no. 1, 1960.

Freeman-Grenville, G. S. P., "Medieval History of the Coast of Tanganyika," Journal of African History, Vol. IV, 1963.

Gray, John, History of Zanzibar, Oxford, London, 1962.

Huntingford, G. W. B., "The Azanian Civilization of Kenya," Antiquity, Vol. VII, no. 6, June, 1933.

Kirkman, John, Men and Monuments, Lutterworth Press, 1964.

Knappert, Jan, "Some Aspects of Swahili Poetry," Tanganyika Notes and Records, no. 55, September, 1960.

Mathew, G. (ed.), History of East Africa, Vol. I and Vol. II, Oxford, London, 1963.

Mathew, G., "Forgotten Cities of the East African Coast," U.N.E.S.C.O. Courier, no. 10, October, 1959.

Oliver, Roland, A review of Historie de Madagascar by Hubert Deschamps, Journal of African History, no. 2, 1960.

Posnansky, Merrick, "Pottery Types from Archaeological Sites in East Africa," Journal of African History, Vol. II, no. 2, 1961.

Posnansky, Merrick, "Pottery Types in East Africa," Journal of African History, Vol. II, no. 2, 1960.

Prins, A. H., The Swahili-speaking Peoples of Zanzibar and the East African Coast, (Ethnographic Survey of East, Central Africa, Part VII), International African Institute, London, 1967.

Trimingham, J. S., Islam in East Africa, Clarendon Press, Oxford London, 1964.

Winstedt, E. O., (ed.), The Christian Typography of Indicopleustes, Cambridge, 1909.

Wrigley, Christopher, "Speculations on the Economic Prehistory
of Africa, " Journal of African History, Vol. I, 1960.

Van Der Steen, E. G. D., "Trade Wind Beads, " Royal Anthropological Institute, Vol. 56, no. 27, February, 1956.

CHAPTER X

Beke, Charles T., On the Countries South of Abyssina, (Royal
Geographical Society Journal), London, 1843.

Burton, Isabel, The Life of Captain Sir Richard F. Burton, London,
1893.

Burton, Richard F., Personal Narrative of a Pilgrimage to Mecca
and El Medina, London, 1855.

Burton, Richard F., (Gordon Waterfield, ed.), "First Footsteps
in East Africa, " London, 1966.

Burton, Richard, F., The Lake Regions of Central Africa, London,
1861.

Burton, Richard F., Zanzibar, London, 1872.

Burton, Richard F., Abeokuta and the Cameroons Mountains,
London, 1863.

Burton, Richard F., (C. W. Newbury, ed.), Mission to King
Gelele of Dahome, London, 1966.

Coupland, Reginald, Kirk on the Zambesi, London, 1928.

Coupland, Reginald, The Exploitation of East Africa, 1856-1898,
London, 1939.

Johnston, Harry H., A History of the Colonization of Africa, New
York, 1966.

Livingstone, David, Missionary Travels and Researches in South Africa, New York, 1868.

Major, Richard Henry, The Discoveries of Prince Henry the Navigator, London, 1877.

MacNair, James, Livingstone's Travels, London, 1954.

Oliver, Roland, The Missionary Factor in East Africa, London, 1952.

Parke, Thomas Heazle, My Personal Experiences in Equatorial Africa, London, 1891.

Perham, Margery, Lugard, The Years of Adventure, 1858-1890, London, 1956.

Perham, Margery, African Discovery, London, 1942.

Rotberg, Robert (ed.), Africa and Its Explorers, Cambridge, 1970.

Schapera, I. (ed.), David Livingstone: Family Letters, 1841-1856, London, 1959.

Seaver, George, David Livingstone: His Life and Letters, New York, 1957.

Simmons, Jack, Livingstone and Africa, London, 1955.

Stanley, Dorothy (ed.), The Autobiography of Sir Henry Morton Stanley, London, 1909.

Stanley, H. M., The Congo and the Founding of Its Free State, London, 1885.

Stanley, H. M., In Darkest Africa, London, 1890.

Thomson, Joseph, To tne Central African Lakes and Back, London, 1891.

Thomson, Joseph, Through Masai Land: A Journey of Exploration among the Snowclad Volcanic Mountains and Strange Tribes of Eastern Equatorial Africa, London, 1883.

Waller, Horace (ed.), The Last Journals of David Livingstone, London, 1874.

Young, Edward Daniel, Report of the Livingstone Search and Expedition (Royal Geographical Society Journal), London, 1868.

*Kush-Journal of the Sudan
Antiquities Service, Khartoum,
The Republic of Sudan

Journal of African History-
School of Oriental and
African Studies, University
of London, England

INDEX

Hall, R. M., 47
Hamitic, 81
Harari, 42
Harrar, 126
Hassan bin Ali, 85
Hassan bin Suleiman, 85
Hellenism, 38, 87
Hehne, 135
Herne, G. E., 126
Herodotus, 22
Hintze, Dr., 25
Hippalus, 79
Husani Kubwa, 89
Huzayyin, Solumon, 7
Hyksos, 20, 21

India, 6, 29, 38, 65, 99, 101,
    102, 106
Indian Ocean, 48, 56, 58, 61, 77,
    79, 83, 96, 97, 102, 111, 137
Indonesia, 1
Inyanga, 65, 66, 67, 68, 74
Islam, 5, 41, 43, 85

Jews, 42
Johnston, Henry Hamilton, 141
Johnston, Keith, Jr., 135
Juba River, 50
Judaism, 42
Judea, 42
Judith, 42, 43
Jur River, 27

Kakuyo Komunyaka, 58, 60
Kalahari Desert, 56, 57, 58, 111
Kamerun, 141
Karanga, 45, 46, 56, 57, 61, 63
Kaole, 128
Kashta, 21
Kavirondo Gulf, 138
Kazeh, 129, 131, 137
Kenya, 40, 50, 60, 78, 81, 82,
    107
Kerma, 20

Khaldun, Ibn, 100
Khami, 63, 64
Khartoum, 2, 15, 19, 25, 37
Kilimanjaro, 137, 141
Kilwa, 5, 62, 78, 82, 83, 84, 85,
    86, 87, 88, 89, 90, 91, 100, 103,
    104, 105, 106, 107, 108, 131
Kinshasa, 141
Kirk, John, 113, 118
Kirkman, Prof., 67, 77
Kisimkazi, 94
Kisimayu, 78
Kiza, Sultan of, 95
Kiza, 95
Kolobeng, 112
Kololo, 111
Kufic, 90
Kumma, 19
Kuruman, 110, 111
Kush, 20, 21, 22, 25
Kushites, 29, 40

Lake Bangweulu, 117
Lake Barengo, 138
Lake Chad, 20
Lake Mweru, 116
Lake Ngami, 111
Lake Nyasa, 114, 115, 116, 134,
    135, 136, 137
Lake Rudolph, 13
Lake Rukwa, 137
Lamu, 84, 108
Land of Punt, 78
Leakey, Dr. Louis, 7, 10, 11, 12,
    13, 76
    Mary (wife), 11, 13
    Richard E. (son), 13
Leopold II, King, 117, 124, 141
Leopolds Kopje, 72
Lepsius, 24, 25
Libyan, 7, 21
Limpopo River, 50, 56, 58, 68,
    69, 72
Linyanti, 111

Livingstone, Charles, 113
Livingstone, Dr. David, 110, 111, 114, 115, 116, 118, 119, 120, 125, 134
London, 131
Lualaba River, 123
Luanda, 111
Lukuga River, 136

Maanyan, 97
MacIver, David Randall, 47
Madagascar, 93, 96, 97, 98
Mafia, 87, 89, 90, 91, 106
Ma'in, 41
Makatuba, 135, 137, 139
Malagasy, 96, 97, 98
Malawi, 67, 114
Malay (s), 96, 97, 98
Mali, Republic of, 15
Malindi, 84, 102, 104, 106
Mambos, 64
Mapungubwe, 68, 69, 70, 71, 72, 74
Masai, 75, 81, 137, 138, 139
Mashona, 64
Massawa, 39
Masudi, 3, 100, 101, 102
Matabele, 46
Mathew, Dr. A.G., 77, 87
Mauch, Carl, 44, 46
Mecca, 125
Medina, 125
Mehenge, 135
Malanin, 16
Merina, 98
Meroë, 1, 2, 8, 15, 19, 20, 21, 22, 23, 24, 25, 26, 27, 28, 29, 30, 31, 32, 34, 35, 36, 38, 49
Meroitic, 31, 33
Mesopotamia, 83, 88
Middle Kingdom, 20
Mikindani, 115
Ming, 82
Mohammed Ali, 24

Mogadishu, 82, 83, 84, 86
Mombasa, 81, 84, 91, 102, 103, 104, 105, 108, 127
Mongol, 88
Monomotapa, 1, 3, 56, 57, 58, 60, 61, 621, 63, 71
Moslem, 37, 41, 83, 100, 109
Mount Elgan, 138
Mount Kenya, 138
Mount Morah, 44
Mount Ngorongoro, 75
Mozambique, 29, 45, 50, 57, 62, 64, 99, 100, 104, 111
Mtelikwi Valley, 48
Murchison, Sir Robert, 114
Murdock, George Peter, 40
Musawwarat es Sofra, 24, 31
Mutota, 57, 58
Mutopa, 58
Mutope, 58
Mwari, 59, 64

Napata (n), 19, 21, 22, 30, 31, 34
Naqa, 30, 34
Narseh, King, 93
Natal, 47
Ndebele, 47
Negro, 15
New Kingdom, 19
Nguni, 47, 54, 68, 115
Nigeria, 37, 140
Nile, 2, 19, 20, 22, 25, 26, 32, 36, 37, 114, 130
Nilotic, 31
Noba - Nobatae, 31
North Africa, 10
Noubai, 36
Nubia, 8, 19, 20, 21, 29
Nubian, 32, 35, 36
Nyahauma, 58
Nyangwe, 116

Ogooue River, 141
Old Kingdom, 19

Olduvai, 6, 7, 10, 11, 12
Oliver, Dr. Roland, 77
Oman, 38, 85, 100, 107
Osiris, 34
Oswell, William Cotton, 111

Pangani estuary, 78
Parke, Thomas H., 119
Pate, 84
Pemba, 78, 85, 93, 94, 103, 106, 107, 108, 127
Periplus, 78
Persians, 41, 80, 82, 83, 84, 85, 91
Philae, 23
Phoenicians, 39
Piankhi, 21
Pleistocene Epoch, 9, 10, 13, 16, 18
Pliny, 23, 25, 77, 81
Pluvial, 9
Portugal, 63
Portuguese, 3, 56, 60, 61, 62, 63, 64, 67, 80, 85, 90, 103, 105, 106, 107, 111, 113
Posnansky, Prof., 29
Posselt, 45
Ptolemy, 78
Punjab, 79

Qataban, 41
Qostol, 35
Quelimane, 111
Quarternary Period, 9

Red Sea, 19, 36, 39, 41, 77, 78
Rhodes, Cecil, 65
Rhodesia, 4, 44, 45, 49, 54, 56, 58, 60, 62, 63, 64, 65, 68, 72, 74, 83
Rift Valley, 6, 10, 75
Robert, Shaaban, 109
Robinson, Keith, 48
Roman, 30, 34, 23, 36, 78, 87

Rome, 23
Rowzi, 3, 54, 56, 57, 59, 62, 63
Ruvuma, 114, 115, 137
Ruzizi River, 117, 130

Sabaens, 38, 40, 47, 78
Sahara, 7, 10, 102
Sassanian, 83
Sawahila, 84
Sekeketu, 111
Semien, 42, 43
Semma, 19
Sena River, 62
Seneca, 23
Senegal, 141
Serengeti Plain, 10
Shabako, 21
Shanakdakhete, Queen, 30
Shapur II, King, 83
Shashi River, 68
Sheba, Queen of, 43, 44
Shiraz, 85, 86, 89, 90, 91
Shiré River, 114
Shona, 3, 45, 46, 54, 59, 64, 65,68
Shurazi, 84, 86
Sierra Leone, 140
Simos, Diago, 63
Sofala, 62, 84, 89, 100, 102, 104, 105
Solomon, King, 43, 44, 100
Somali, 81, 82, 86, 126
Somalia, 78, 82
Somalialand, 82, 126
Sonjo, 76
Song Marna, 87, 88
Sotho, 73
Spain, 37
Speke, John H., 114, 126, 127, 128, 129, 130, 131, 132, 134
Stanley, Henry Morton, 110, 116, 117, 118, 119, 120, 121, 122, 123, 124, 125, 134, 141
Stillbay, 80
Stone Age, 15, 29, 74